LEADERSHIP

Essential Steps Every Manager Needs to Know
Third Edition

Elwood N. Chapman

Sharon Lund O'Neil

University of Houston

Prentice Hall
Upper Saddle River, NJ 07458

Library of Congress Cataloging-in-Publication Data

Chapman, Elwood N.
    Leadership : essential steps every manager needs to know / Elwood
N. Chapman, Sharon Lund O'Neil. —3rd ed.
      p.   cm.
    Includes index.
    ISBN 0-13-010019-6
    1. Leadership. I. O'Neil, Sharon Lund. II. Title.
  HD57.7C47 1999
  658.4'092—dc21
                                                       99-14824
                                                       CIP

Acquisition editor: Elizabeth Sugg
Editorial/production supervision, interior design,
  and electronic page makeup: Mary Araneo
Interior art: Don Martinetti
Manufacturing buyer: Ed O'Dougherty
Cover designer: Bruce Kenselaar
Cover director: Jayne Conte
Managing editor: Mary Carnis
Marketing manager: Shannon Simonsen
Director of manufacturing and production: Bruce Johnson
Printer/binder: Victor Graphics

© 2000, 1989 by Prentice-Hall, Inc.
Upper Saddle River, NJ 07458

Previously published under the title *Leadership: What Every Manager Needs to Know* by
Elwood N. Chapman and *Put More Leadership into Your Style* by Elwood N. Chapman,
copyright ©1984 by Science Research Associates, Inc.

Printed in the United States of America

10 9 8 7 6 5

ISBN 0-13-010019-6

PRENTICE-HALL INTERNATIONAL (UK) LIMITED, *London*
PRENTICE-HALL OF AUSTRALIA PTY. LIMITED, *Sydney*
PRENTICE-HALL CANADA INC., *Toronto*
PRENTICE-HALL HISPANOAMERICANA, S.A., *Mexico*
PRENTICE-HALL OF INDIA PRIVATE LIMITED, *New Delhi*
PRENTICE-HALL OF JAPAN, INC., *Tokyo*
PEARSON ASIA PTE. LTD., *Singapore*
EDITORA PRENTICE-HALL DO BRASIL, LTDA., *Rio de Janeiro*

There go my people.
I must find out
where they are going
so I can lead them.

Alexandre Ledru-Rollin
1807–1874

Contents

Exercises

Preface

Leadership has taken on new meaning as leaders around the world are "studied," evaluated, and compared for their effectiveness. Scholars generally recognize that there is a serious leadership gap in America. Although most noticeable in the political and business arenas, the gap is also recognized in all types of organizations including educational, governmental, religious, youth, and volunteer organizations.

As valuable as it may be, management training alone is not enough to eliminate the leadership gap. What is needed is a wide variety of leadership training programs at all levels.

This book, *Leadership: Essential Steps Every Manager Needs to Know*, is designed to meet the needs of four educational and training areas:

1. Basic textbook for leadership courses:

Formal courses on leadership development have gained a high profile on many college campuses, in business schools and institutes, with religious and volunteer groups, and in the corporate training world. Courses with a focus on closing the leadership gap are popular and will continue to grow in prominence. The book can be used by educators and trainers in variety of settings for a stand-alone leadership course.

2. Special unit within traditional management/other courses:

Many outstanding management textbooks do not adequately cover the subject of leadership. Instructors of management, human relations, communications, self-improvement, and career development can use the book as a special unit to expand their courses. Many professors are already supplementing their favorite management texts with shorter, less expensive books to cover the topic of leadership. A typical leadership unit can last several class periods, and it frequently extends from two to six weeks.

3. Community workshops, training seminars, and leadership retreats:

The book is appropriate for many types of workshops and seminars that are aimed at leadership development and improvement. Persons conducting continuing and distance education programs as well as those already in community leadership roles realize the need for programs to help people become more effective and productive. Individuals who study the essentials of leadership are those who contribute to their own self-worth, as well as to organizational goals.

4. Individual study and self-motivation:

The format and style (exercises, cases, self-tests) make the book ideal for self-study. These features also make it suitable when classroom time is limited or formal classes are not available. In addition, readers who are cognizant of the need for self-improvement can study and apply the essentials of leadership at their own pace and in their own settings. The presentation of the leadership essentials gives the reader variety as well as flexibility in applying the material.

Acknowledgments

Portions of *Leadership: Essential Steps Every Manager Needs to Know* first appeared in *Put More Leadership into Your Style,* 1984, and later in *Leadership: What Every Manager Needs to Know,* 1989. The original work was based on 60 interviews with a wide spectrum of recognized leaders.

Over the years the material for *Leadership: Essential Steps Every Manager Needs to Know* has been verified, revised, and strengthened from additional interviews, observations, classes, seminars, and workshops. Other changes have been made as a result of critiques from professors, corporate trainers, and community leaders who used the book in their programs.

We wish to thank all those involved for their contributions.

Sharon Lund O'Neil

To the Student

Leadership: Essential Steps Every Manager Needs to Know has four special features:

1. The Leadership Formula (Leadership Strategic Model) presents the fundamentals or basic elements designed to fit into your present style, no matter what role you play or what position you occupy. You can use the model as a guide to your leadership growth; you can discover and strengthen weak areas in your style; and you can use the model to rate others on their leadership skills.

2. The book is full of exercises, tests, and assessments that will help you adopt and practice what you learn as you go. As you weave leadership into your present style, you will enhance your ability to lead. The book should be read with a pencil in hand.

3. Each of the ten chapters in the book represent an essential of leadership. Note that the title of each chapter begins with an action verb. Whatever your level of leadership ability, the key to improving your skills is to take action.

4. At the end of each chapter, there are two cases that you are invited to complete. Compare your responses to those of the authors (found at the back of the book). While ideal for group discussions, the cases are also beneficial when the book is used as a self-study or self-improvement text.

Enjoy your adventure into the challenging world of leadership!

About the Authors

Elwood N. Chapman, co-author of *Leadership: Essential Steps Every Manager Needs to Know* and author of several other books, was known as "Mr. Attitude" in California until his death in 1995. He was praised for his friendly writing style and practical advice, which reflected his lifelong interest in the style and substance of the business world. A graduate of the University of California at Berkeley and former professor at Chaffey College, "Chap" was a nationally-known consultant and a popular speaker.

Sharon Lund O'Neil, co-author of *Leadership: Essential Steps Every Manager Needs to Know*, is a widely published author and the recipient of numerous teaching and leadership awards. Her human relations cases, based on the corporate work environment, are popular with both trainers and educators. She has a common-sense approach to problem solving—an approach she has practiced as a leader of several national professional organizations. She holds a Ph.D. degree from the University of Illinois and is currently a professor at the University of Houston.

1 ★ Develop Your Freedom to Lead

Managers are the maintenance people of business.

Adrian Chalfant

⭐ 1 Develop Your Freedom to Lead

MANAGEMENT PLUS LEADERSHIP SPELL SUCCESS

Leadership is the ability to influence others, especially in getting others to reach challenging goals. So how do leaders influence others? Some leaders use their charisma and charm. For other leaders, enthusiasm and excitement are their main assets. Others may use a good knowledge base and intelligence. And for still others, strength and bravery may be the way they influence followers. There are many leadership traits. But, without a doubt, to be a leader, it is quite important to win the respect and admiration of followers and peers. And understanding others is probably the best way to help yourself as well as others reach personal and professional goals.

If you think a leadership role is beyond your reach, think again. It may not be—because your leadership potential is probably greater than you ever anticipated. Also, there are almost as many leadership opportunities as there are potential leaders. Some may be so close to you that you cannot see them.

Think of this book, then, as a road map that will lead you to understand the essence of leadership—and as a guide that will help you organize the skills and traits you already have into a marketable leadership package.

DO YOU HAVE THE RIGHT STUFF?

You need not have a particular combination of skills and personality traits to lead others. In fact, no one, including psychologists and management experts, has been able to develop a theory which proves that leadership is merely the result of the right combination of personal characteristics. The experts identify so many acceptable traits—and mixes—that almost anyone can qualify. In other words, you are not automatically disqualified as a potential leader because you feel uncomfortable at large parties or because you prefer reading to playing handball.

This is not to say that you should not make the most of what you have. You should certainly capitalize on your strengths, skills, and the positive personality traits you already possess.

Please take a moment to complete the simple exercise, "Leadership Characteristics I Respect," that follows.

WHERE ARE THE LEADERSHIP OPPORTUNITIES?

Everywhere! There are many more leadership opportunities than you may suspect. If you think you are ready for a leadership role, there is probably one waiting for you now.

It is a very common phenomenon that in all businesses the farther one goes up the organizational ladder, the harder it is to find people who qualify for the demanding leadership positions near or at the top. There may be an abundance of leaders at lower levels, but most fall by the wayside before they get close to the top. Some are promoted beyond their level of competency (the Peter Principle) and climb no further; some lose their motivation to become leaders and opt for pure management roles; and some of those who do rise to the top in the business world may become so valuable that competitive organizations lure them away.

There are also opportunities and critical needs for leaders in other areas—unions, youth organizations, churches, and community volunteer groups. The leadership shortage you read about is real and is accelerating at a fast pace. And there is no reason why you should not take advantage of it.

LEADERSHIP CHARACTERISTICS I RESPECT

From the following list of characteristics (traits or behaviors) write out the five you respect most in a leader. Also, add or substitute characteristics you feel are needed to complete the list.

Patient	Charismatic	Self-motivated	Organized
Compassionate	Good communicator	Calm under pressure	Competent
Inspirational	Firm	Visionary	Optimistic
Decisive	Fair	Strong-willed	Flexible
Integrity	Knowledgeable	Resourceful	Humor
Objective	Open	Team builder	Realistic
Positive attitude	Consistent	Even-tempered	Coach
High energy	Innovative	Enthusiastic	Genuine
Tactful	Ambitious	Delegator	Risk-taker
Dependable	Efficient	Negotiator	Persistent
Goal Oriented	Fearless	Productive	Change agent

My preferences:

1. _____

2. _____

3. _____

4. _____

5. _____

You may wish to return to this list to make changes after you have completed the book.

MANAGEMENT VERSUS LEADERSHIP

Writers have been trying for years to explain the real difference between management and leadership. It is not an easy task, because the two areas are so closely interwoven.

In general, management is concerned with achieving organizational objectives. Management means planning, organizing, communicating, controlling, and evaluating. It means resolving conflicts. It means setting goals and helping move employees toward them.

Management is keeping people productive, maintaining optimal working conditions, and making the best possible use of all resources. Also, management is anticipating problems and solving them before productivity declines. It is holding things together as well as moving things forward, usually with the goal of utilizing resources in a cost effective manner.

All of these tasks, of course, involve some degree of leadership. But leadership is not synonymous with management.

COMPARING MANAGERS WITH LEADERS

The differences between an excellent leader and a successful manager are subtle and difficult to define. Sometimes a manager is a leader in one or two areas, but not enough to make an impact. Others start by extending themselves (stepping out in front) in a few instances and then, as their confidence grows, venturing further into leadership roles. While most people move from management into leadership positions in a haphazard, uncharted manner, more and more emphasis is being placed on leadership training. Helping you to understand leadership styles and to develop your own leadership skills is the purpose of this book.

Please complete the following exercise which compares manager and leader traits and skills. Once you have fully analyzed the Leadership Formula in Chapter 3, you will be more insightful in making a comparison of managers and leaders.

If, at this stage, you question the validity of the comparison, place a check in the appropriate square.

Managers	*Leaders*	*Questionable*
Protect their operations	Advance their operations	☐
Accept responsibility	Seek responsibility	☐
Minimize risks	Take calculated risks	☐
Accept speaking opportunities	Generate speaking opportunities	☐
Set reasonable goals	Set "unreasonable" goals	☐
Pacify problem employees	Challenge problem employees	☐
Strive for a comfortable working environment	Strive for an exciting working environment	☐
Use power cautiously	Use power forcefully	☐
Delegate cautiously	Delegate enthusiastically	☐
View workers as employees	View workers as potential followers	☐

A manager may develop the perfect strategy to make an organization successful, but unless he or she also is a leader, the strategy will fail. Leadership, then, takes a bigger, broader view. Leadership takes you into new territory where change, risk, vision, creativity, and challenge become ingrained in your everyday working style. As a manager, you may be content to work primarily inside the framework of your organization. As a leader, you become increasingly concerned with the direction the organization is taking. As a manager, you may be satisfied to follow the lead of high-level personnel. As a leader, you prepare yourself to become a member of the group that leads the way. In the pursuit of excellence, a manager developing as a leader plays a bigger and bigger leadership role.

Mark and Maria have a lot going for them. He is the new city manager in their community of over 60,000 residents; she is the principal of the local high school. They have an excellent combined income, a lovely home, and both are still under 40 years of age.

MANAGEMENT SKILLS: A PREREQUISITE FOR LEADERSHIP

Mark has built his career on a sound educational foundation—an undergraduate degree in business administration and a masters in public administration. He acquired his management skills early. He knows how to plan, organize, control, delegate, appraise, and set priorities. He is an expert on public finance and data processing. Because Mark has perfected his management skills, he has more time to develop his role as a leader.

Maria, too, has a good educational background. She earned a teacher education degree, taught high school science for several years, and worked her way into a leadership position through leadership practice. That is, instead of studying management as Mark had done, she demonstrated her managerial and leadership ability by heading several faculty committees; then she was appointed chairperson of her department. Sensing the direction her career was taking, she returned to graduate school to earn a degree in educational leadership and administration.

The point is not how or when Mark and Maria received their management and leadership training and experience. The important thing is that, because they have become efficient managers, they found it was important to improve their leadership skills. They have gained the background they need for more demanding future leadership roles.

Management training or experience is the best foundation on which to build a successful leadership role. But as important as management training or experience is, acquiring *management* skills is not a substitute for developing *leadership* skills. The blend of the two provides the winning combination.

There is long-standing debate as to whether leaders are "born" or are "made." Certainly there is good merit in researching the arguments for both views to gain a better understanding of the leadership challenge you face. The authors believe, however, that without a doubt, leadership

ARE YOU READY TO ACCEPT THE LEADERSHIP CHALLENGE?

can be developed. Having a good attitude, understanding people, accepting others' views, and working at building interpersonal relationships—all play an important role in the development of leadership skills.

As a leader, you will still use many management skills, but you will add a new dimension to your responsibilities. You will start to change your image from a maintenance person to a mover and shaker, from a data giver to a data user, from a decision follower to a decision maker, from a manager who *works with* employees to one who *empowers* people and builds teams.

The transition from management to leadership may appear to be subtle, but when it happens, it doesn't take long for others to notice the change. There is an interesting twist, almost a paradox, to the entire management-leadership dichotomy. It goes like this:

> **YOU CAN BE AN EXCELLENT MANAGER WITHOUT BECOMING A GOOD LEADER; BUT YOU CANNOT BE AN EXCELLENT LEADER WITHOUT BECOMING A GOOD MANAGER.**

For the most part, the above statement is true. Good management skills provide not only the foundation for good leadership, but also (in most cases) the time to lead. You simply cannot become a strong leader until the management side of the operation is running smoothly.

Making the transition from a management position requires commitment. Even for experienced managers, acquiring new leadership skills is not an overnight proposition. The reason one must make a commitment is that leadership involves a state of mind. You must *want* to become a leader before changes can occur.

Another, more powerful reason a leadership commitment is important is found in the danger of becoming a "management marshmallow." To explain, one must understand that managing a firm, a department, a team, a school, or a government agency always involves a mass of details. There are procedures to follow, reports to write, controls to cross-check, human relations differences to handle, etc. Administrative work is not always exciting, but it is necessary. How else can plans be implemented and productivity measured? Frequently, however, managers permit themselves to become so immersed in managerial functions that they cannot see the leadership "forest" for the management "trees." Thus, administrative work can draw managers deeper and deeper into the "management marshmallow"—the soft, comfortable, gooey cloud of detail that keeps them from seeing the big picture.

To lead, one must look beyond the familiar pleasures of routine work. Unfortunately, some managers are unable to do so.

The Upward Mobility Leadership Expansion Principle states that those who want to move up must reduce the time spent on administrative matters and expand the time devoted to leadership. The principle implies that those who fail to make the transition into leadership fast enough may be passed over. Generally speaking, beginning supervisors should devote the vast majority of their time to management activities. But when they move into the next level of management, the reverse should be true. Leadership ability, not management ability, is the primary criterion for upward mobility.

A corollary to this theory: The sooner an individual demonstrates leadership skills at the bottom of the ladder, the sooner he or she begins to move up. The reverse also is true: the longer that person waits, the more likely it is that she or he will be left behind in a minor management role.

Most people—but not all—move into leadership roles from management positions. Some make the transition as students, homemakers, or community volunteers. These individuals do not have to fight the "management marshmallow" problem. But in order to survive, they need to learn management skills as they go along. Learning how to delegate, set priorities, manage time, and so on, must be mastered at the same time they are incorporating leadership skills into their style. It is a dual responsibility.

HOW STYMIED ARE LEADERS WITHOUT MANAGEMENT TRAINING?

The director of athletics at a large college views the problem this way: "I'm glad I was a successful coach before I took over this job because I was able to develop most of my leadership skills before I arrived. But I have learned to respect management skills. My transition would have been much easier if I had taken some management courses earlier."

Just as we have excellent managers with little leadership ability, we have some leaders who are weak managers. Some are so good at leadership that their lack of management skills is overlooked. The management function in many situations may be minimal, especially if a person's leadership ability is so strong that others assume the managerial duties. Some leaders (politicians, film producers, coaches) may be so good that their poor management skills can be ignored or at least tolerated. There are also cases where the powers that be will provide a good manager to act as a backstop for an exceptional leader. Good leaders are much harder to find than good managers. (And managers usually are paid less.)

ARE THERE SUCCESSFUL LEADERS WHO ARE WEAK MANAGERS?

Still, any leader who is not also a good manager is always vulnerable. Having poor organization skills will undermine the leader's authority and may eventually contribute to her or his collapse. As much as subordinates may value a person's leadership qualities, they still like to work or play in a nonchaotic environment.

It always works both ways.

Successful leaders, without adequate management skills, should protect themselves by developing their skills. One way to gain management skills is by enrolling in a management training program. Successful managers who want to become more than administrators should avail themselves of any leadership training opportunities that may be available.

One complements the other.

HOW MUCH TIME DO TOP MANAGERS DEVOTE TO LEADERSHIP?

Having interviewed numerous top leaders, it was interesting to find how most felt about the time they spend on management vs. leadership. Only two stated firmly that virtually all of their time was devoted to leadership efforts. A few indicated that a majority of their time was spent on what they termed *leadership* matters, but most said that they devoted far more time to management than to leadership. The most interesting finding, however, was that all wanted to free themselves to spend more time on leadership.

One president of a major firm in Boston stated: "I doubt that I spend even half of my time on leadership matters, but it isn't because I don't want to. I find there are always fires for me to put out; usually problems that my managers can't handle. This means I must put on my management hat and continue to wear it until things are squared away. You might interpret this to be a reflection on my lack of management ability, but I believe it is something all corporate heads must deal with."

Ideally, leaders at the very top should spend no more than about 20 percent of their time on management and about 80 percent on leadership. Reality, of course, can dictate otherwise. The percentage of time devoted to leadership gradually drops for those in less responsible positions. This should not be interpreted to mean that first-line managers should be satisfied with the limited time they spend on leadership, nor that the work they do is unimportant. In any case, they should constantly strive to improve their effectiveness, keeping in mind that the better they are at management, the more time they will have to devote to leadership.

To help you summarize your thoughts pertaining to this chapter, complete the following important read-and-respond exercise.

READ-AND-RESPOND: MANAGERS VS. LEADERS

Throughout this book you will be encouraged to compare and analyze the functions and styles of managers and leaders. In the end, you will make your own evaluation and decide just how much leadership to put into *your* management style (or how much management to put into your leadership style). This exercise is designed to start you thinking in this direction.

Instructions: Read each paragraph, check the appropriate box, and respond with a few words of your own in the spaces provided.

Managers

A manager maintains an efficient operation through the effective use of available resources of all kinds. Tasks include budgeting, preparation of financial statements, creating and maintaining good relationships with people, delegating, appraising results, preparing production quotas and sales plans, organizing and analyzing data, setting priorities, planning, controlling functions, and resolving human conflict. Managers control more than they create. Superior in operational matters, successful managers take great pride in quality performance and consistency. Their goal is productivity and profit within their territory.

There is no such thing as a "pure manager." Some degree of leadership is involved in all management roles. Those who come close to being 100-percent managers often operate branch offices away from headquarters operations. Leadership comes from the home office. Some managers shun leadership roles. They prefer the status quo and get their rewards from maintaining a productive, profitable operation. To them, the road to higher management is better management.

Agree　　*Disagree*
☐　　　　☐

My Comments: _____

_____

_____

_____

Manager/Leaders

Manager/leaders function first as managers, then as leaders. They feel that good management and all it entails will free them to lead. Management, to many of these people, is a backup or foundation operation, allowing them to achieve improvements (even greater productivity) through innovative leadership. Management is "tending the store" whereas leadership is stepping in front to speed progress. Manager/leaders are satisfied to be managers first and leaders second because it minimizes the risks of being leaders. If they "get burned" trying something new, they can fall back on their management track record. Many have the attitude that good management qualifies them for promotions, but leadership gets them there.

Organizational leaders are more apt to come from marketing, sales, and public relations departments than from production or accounting.

Agree ☐   Disagree ☐

My Comments: _____

_____

_____

_____

Leaders

There is no such thing as a "pure leadership" position. All leaders in all roles must assume some management functions. Even if a leader is successful in delegating all management functions to others, delegating is management. Here are two examples of the mix: An outstanding coach may be 90 percent leader, but he or she must still deal with eligibility, backup services, and other management problems. A politician may be successful because of his or her leadership qualities, but not all management functions can be turned over to a campaign manager. Most coaches and politicians would benefit from a management course.

Agree ☐   Disagree ☐

My Comments: _____

_____

_____

_____

Leader/Managers

A leader/manager goes as far as possible in delegating management functions to others, as long as efficiency is not sacrificed. Leaders know the value of having a smooth operation behind them. Some of the most successful leaders in all environments "manage" to become 75 percent leaders and 25 percent managers. No small achievement! Sometimes those who move too quickly in their leadership roles have to fall back and pick up the pieces.

Most individuals who move into upper management go through the transition from primarily management roles into primarily leadership roles. How far they go depends upon the type of organization as well as their leadership abilities. Most successful CEOs are more leaders than managers. But not all. In the military, officers and platoon sergeants are often excellent examples of leader/managers. Youth leaders (YMCA, scouting, church groups) also fall into this category.

Agree ☐   Disagree ☐

My Comments: _____

_____

_____

_____

* Leadership is the ability to influence others, especially toward challenging goals.

* Management skills constitute the best background for successful leadership; they should never be neglected.

* Management skills, however, do not replace leadership skills.

* Managers may have an ideal strategic plan for an organization to be successful; but, without leadership, the plan will fail.

* You can be an excellent manager without becoming a good leader, but (except in rare cases) you cannot be an excellent leader without becoming a good manager.

* Managers can increase their chances for upward mobility by devoting more time to developing their leadership skills.

* Successful leaders who are short on management skills can enhance their career options and become less vulnerable with additional management training.

SUMMARY

Case 1: Controversy

Professor Adams is the highly respected dean of the business school at the state university. He has written three management books. His faculty is considered the most capable and experienced in the Northwest. Two years ago Dr. Adams submitted a request to the curriculum committee to initiate a new course in leadership for all students on campus. The committee finally approved the request. But Dr. Rosen, dean of instruction, does not feel the course should be taught in the business school. She argues: "I believe management professors, no matter how capable, are so far into the management forest that they cannot see the leadership trees. I'm not sure they can treat the subject objectively. After all, we need political, community, and religious leaders every bit as much as we need good business leaders. If we offer the course in the social science department, we will attract more students from these disciplines. There is, as you know, a great need to train our own student leaders on this campus. I doubt if many of them would enroll in a business course."

Dr. Adams is most upset by this turn of events. His counter-arguments are:

"A good management background is essential to good leadership. They cannot be separated. Several of our professors would do an outstanding job of teaching the subject—they have demonstrated strong leadership skills themselves through service in the college, professional organizations, and community groups. They know management and currently teach the development of leadership traits and skills in their courses. Students preparing for nonbusiness leadership roles will benefit immeasurably from the management orientation they will receive. We guarantee that we will deal effectively with the subject of leadership in all areas of society. The course would not have, as Dr. Rosen implies, a total business orientation."

Whom would you support in the controversy? What other arguments would you submit from either side? Why, in your opinion, do many colleges neglect the important subject of leadership? (For the authors' reactions, turn to the back of the book.)

Samantha and her husband, Elgin, frequently discuss their careers and their futures over after-dinner coffee. Elgin, an MBA, is a middle manager in a large oil company. Although bored with the job he now holds (because it does not make use of his capabilities), Elgin believes that his training in management theory will eventually spring him into a high-level leadership position with his firm.

Samantha is a successful youth leader. Her national organization frequently asks her to conduct leadership workshops. She feels that she has already mastered much of what there is to know about leadership. She also believes that her leadership experiences constitute the best launching pad into higher positions. At Elgin's suggestion, Samantha is taking her first course in management at a local college.

"Elgin, I believe I have a real edge on the others in my class who are also seeking administrative positions. I think my record as a successful leader puts me at a definite advantage. As soon as I get a few management techniques under my belt, I'm ready to move. I won't have to learn leadership techniques once I get my first administrative opportunity."

"You'd be better off, Sam, if you had more management expertise before you moved into leadership. Management is the foundation of leadership. You've put the cart before the horse. Right now you are underestimating the importance of management and overestimating what you know about leadership. I suggest you get a degree in management, and then perhaps some of your leadership experience will give you a slight advantage."

"Come off it, Elgin. You have been so brainwashed by your management training that you can't think straight. You talk management, management, management. You never even use the word "leadership." I'm already a leader, so I will never fall so deeply into the management trap that I'll lose sight of what organizations really need. If you really knew what I'm talking about, you would not be boxed into that position you hate."

Who do you feel has the better background for future success—Elgin, with his excellent management foundation, or Samantha, with her successful leadership experiences? Defend your position. (The authors' views are listed in the back of the book.)

Self-Test

Mark each statement True (T) or False (F).

___ 1. There is no such thing as a "pure leadership" position.

___ 2. Management skills constitute part of the substance clearly needed to back up a successful leadership style.

___ 3. Management skills are not a substitute for leadership skills.

___ 4. Those who aspire to be leaders, but do not have management backgrounds, can learn management techniques along with leadership skills.

___ 5. You can become an excellent manager and not be a good leader.

___ 6. You must be in upper management before you can put more leadership in your style.

___ 7. The Upward Mobility Leadership Expansion Principle says that those seeking to move higher in their organizations should reduce the time spent on administrative matters and expand the time devoted to leadership.

___ 8. Some successful leaders are poor managers.

___ 9. Leaders can never get completely away from their management responsibilities.

___ 10. Leader/managers are more successful than manager/leaders.

Turn to the back of the book to check your answers.

TOTAL CORRECT _____

2 Mobilize Potential for Higher Productivity

There are an enormous number of managers who have retired on the job.

Peter Drucker

⭐ 2 Mobilize Potential for Higher Productivity

CLOSING PRODUCTIVITY GAPS

Viewed from a broad and distant perspective, the purpose of both management and leadership training is higher personal and group productivity. Productivity is conceived as: higher quality and quantity in tangible goods (e.g., automobiles); more pleasant and efficient customer treatment, resulting in higher sales (e.g., in restaurants); and better performance per tax dollar spent in government (library, postal service, military, etc.).

Good management can go a long way in closing productivity gaps in any organization. Assume, for example, that an organization or department is not effectively managed. As a result, the productivity gap is wide, as illustrated below.

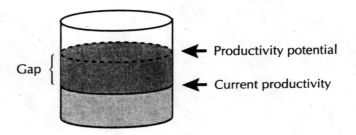

If a new manager (with greater skills) were to take over and were given adequate time, substantial progress could be made toward closing the gap, moving productivity closer to the potential level.

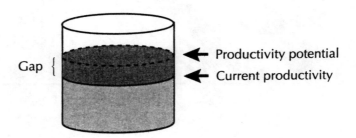

Good management pays off as far as productivity is concerned. But can management alone (with all of the best strategies, controls, people techniques, etc.) get as close to the potential level as it is possible to achieve? Or does it also require a high level of leadership?

It is the premise of this book that if the Leadership Formula (Chapter 3) is absorbed and followed by an excellent manager, further closing of the productivity gap can be anticipated. Just how much the gap can be closed will depend upon how much leadership is added and how skillfully it is applied. It is not unusual that leaders seem

1. to create changes that lead to higher productivity,

2. to motivate their people from a better perspective, thus gaining more productivity, and

3. to put all facets of the "productive machine" together better, so that greater productivity is achieved.

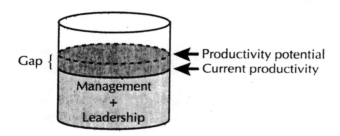

For these reasons, leadership training is recommended as an integral (but separate) part of management training. Although application of the Leadership Formula (the body of this book) is the key to supplementing management with leadership, seven important factors which describe effective leaders deserve consideration here.

LEADERS ARE STRONG MOTIVATORS

Some managers are unable to motivate their people to reach higher standards of personal productivity because they are enmeshed in the management marshmallow. They are more efficiency and control oriented than goal oriented. They dwell more on cost savings than on human motivation. While this is going on, the good manager/leader (following the Leadership Formula) helps employees by empowering them to reach their potential. Thus, the employees become followers—motivated by the leader—and their gains result in higher productivity from each individual.

Frequently an increase in one person's individual productivity is a motivator for other employees on the team. When the team experiences an increase in its overall productivity as a result of increased individual efforts, the work unit usually becomes stronger. The result in greater productivity from the total team effort is frequently referred to as a positive residual, or synergy, which contributes to the "whole being greater than the sum of its parts". That is, the increased individual efforts positively affect the total team productivity. The leader's efforts then have not only increased each of the followers' contributions to the whole, but have built the whole into an enhanced team.

It should be apparent, then, that the difference between supervising an employee and empowering a follower is critical to higher productivity. An employee wants to survive and progress through personal productivity; a follower wants to achieve the same goal as the leader so she or he can share in the victory. Here are two examples:

> Jack is a prototype of the excellent manager. He is steady, efficient, sensitive to the needs of employees, and goal oriented. He involves his people in decision making, provides a comfortable work environment, and gains respect along with productivity. Upper management likes Jack.

> Gary is also an excellent manager (much the same as Jack), but he has a different attitude toward goals. He sets goals that are more inspirational and difficult to achieve, and then uses his personality power to the hilt to make progress. Whether his team reaches the goals is not important; the productivity created in the attempt is the key.

What is the real difference between Jack and Gary? People work for Jack. People follow Gary. When you follow a leader, you are apt to be pulled in the direction of the leader's goals. The difference is subtle, but it often manifests itself in greater productivity.

LEADERS ARE RISK TAKERS

Many successful managers do not want to stick their necks out or "rock the boat" because they believe a smooth, consistent operation is more productive over the long run. These managers personify the "steady as you go" attitude. Most feel they can "manage" their people into higher productivity through sensitivity and good human relations. And many are extremely successful at doing this. A comparison of the following two illustrations will communicate the difference.

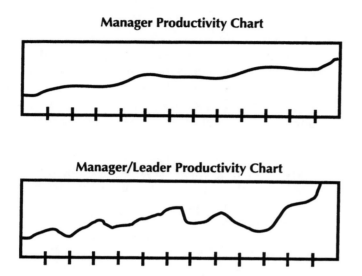

Manager Productivity Chart

Manager/Leader Productivity Chart

Note from the manager productivity chart that the progress of the team is somewhat steady and upward. In contrast is the manager/leader productivity chart. Note that productivity also is upward, but because progress is more sporadic, the end result is higher. Because the leader takes more risks in his or her operation, the climb may not be steady (leaders initiate changes that are often temporarily disruptive to people) but the long-run productivity gain can be higher. Here's why.

1. Leaders do not wait around expecting time alone to solve sticky human relations problems. They gather the facts, assess the situation, then act. Leaders may not make everybody happy, but they are willing to confront the few to motivate the majority.

2. Leaders do not stall until they can make a fail-safe decision. They listen to staff members, tie what they hear to productivity goals, and make a firm decision. If necessary, a "gut" decision often will do.

3. Leaders do not ignore, but do not burden themselves with, details and small decisions. Rather, they delegate them so they are free to work on the big picture, make important decisions, and move on to greater things.

LEADERS ARE DECISIVE

Successful leaders work at honing their thinking and decision-making skills. Being able to separate the small issues from large ones helps leaders make sound, quick decisions. It is no easy task, however. Leaders have learned they must be thorough, but still only gather the important facts. With so much information readily available to people today, it is the leader/manager who has the right information at the right time who usually has the competitive edge.

Timeliness is also an important skill that goes hand in hand with decisiveness. For informed decision making to take place in a timely manner, leaders must learn to separate insignificant facts from the important ones. While a manager may be responsible for carrying out an important decision, leaders frequently must put their necks on the line to make crucial decisions. Many leaders have found the best way to learn this skill is to work at developing their thinking and decision-making abilities. One of the best activities which expands your thinking ability is reading. Working word puzzles and doing two or more activities simultaneously (even watching two TV programs at the same time) can stimulate thinking and also will develop better thinking power.

Because reading is such an important activity for expanding the mind, many successful leaders read continually. Reading a wide variety of materials also is recommended. Some top leaders have suggested reading books, magazines, and newspapers that are totally out of their career areas just to expand their perspectives and ideas of things.

Leaders who are good decision makers also are those who like to dream, set lofty goals, and explore strategies and alternatives. Having a dream can be a tremendous challenge to motivate you to action. Goal setting follows the same rule—most people will tell you that there is more fun in life while working toward goals than in the actual reality when the goals are reached.

Leaders enjoy problem solving challenges. A "what if" approach to problem solving is a popular technique that many leaders employ—individually and with their work teams. Leaders like to get the opinions of their followers. Leaders value the judgment of those who give serious thought to problem solving. Do you enjoy being part of a decision making process? Can you improve your skills in this area? Keep in mind that strategic thinking is a skill that can be developed with practice. In fact, most leadership abilities are sharpened with training, practice, and use. It's up to you to decide on what areas you want to concentrate to improve your leadership skills.

LEADERS ASK FOR MORE RESPONSIBILITY

A good manager may be satisfied to wait until her or his superiors delegate more responsibility, based upon a high-performance record. A good leader will see something that needs to be done and ask for the responsibility to do it. Leaders step out in front. They are not intimidated by superiors. They seek new arenas of responsibility so they can demonstrate their leadership and attract more followers. Leaders are not concerned about being overworked. They assume a new responsibility, delegate an old one, and move on.

Do leaders create their own "kingdoms"?

In some respects, yes. But not always for their self-esteem or power. Often they seek additional responsibilities to gain more control over productivity so they can set new records. Leaders are the first to admit that their long-range future depends upon performance. Without higher productivity, a leader can lose upper management support, as well as his or her followers. Either way, the game is soon over.

Just as leaders like to take on more responsibility, they also want change. The status quo is boring and uncomfortable for true leaders. Leaders can readily be singled out because they do not enjoy remaining static. They are innovators, change agents, and risk takers. You may not find these concepts settling because most people find comfort zones in doing what is expected of them and finding common ground to do it. But skills associated with change and innovation also can be learned. Frequently, a leader can be distinguished from a manager with the degree of success that has been accomplished in fostering change.

LEADERS DRIVE CHANGE

Most successful leaders are challenged by change. While some like "change for change's sake," most others will develop a plan—no matter how sketchy—and not just shoot from the hip. Change without direction is not much value. And ideas without implementation plans can be foolish and even dangerous. Good leaders know that there must be some type of game plan—and frequently they are the ones to develop it.

Communication is one of the most important skills of a leader. If a leader is not able to communicate with his or her followers, the best strategy or plan is lost. Leaders also know there are many components of communication that must be fostered—written communication, the spoken word, nonverbal expression—in addition to development of presentation skills, listening skills, and a positive attitude.

LEADERS ARE GOOD COMMUNICATORS

Leaders know that communication can make or break them. They also know that their communication effectiveness is directly proportional to their attitudes. In fact, 90 to 92 percent of your daily communication is based on your attitude. In Chapter 4 the essential elements of good communication will be discussed. But a brief discussion of the importance of a positive attitude as the root of good communication and a leader's overall success is appropriate here.

LEADERS HAVE POSITIVE ATTITUDES

Positive people think positive thoughts, do positive things, and attract positive people. Successful leaders have perfected this characteristic to work to their advantage. Leaders know that their attitudes belong to them. They are the persons others want to follow; they are the ones who make a difference.

Leaders empower their attitudes. That is, they understand that a positive attitude can make or break a tense situation. They know that the negativism in our society is continuing to grow and is having damaging effects in all corners of life. They know that in this environment keeping a positive attitude is not easy, but it is the key to the development of most of the other traits and skills that are so important for good leadership.

Five of the most important attitude empowerment elements* are listed here. See how many of them you can rate "high" if you look at your attitude right now:

1. See Things from a Positive Perspective. Do you see things that are right with a situation? Do you give other people the benefit of the doubt? The best way for a person to become more positive is by thinking positive thoughts and doing positive things. Today's challenges force people into having to work at being positive. That's okay because positive people also are more enthusiastic about life.

2. Place a High Value on Your Attitude. A leader's attitude is his or her most valuable possession. Leaders who place high values on their attitudes are less likely to get their attitudes stepped on by other people. And a person who respects him or herself and truly values her or his own positive attitude needs to consciously protect his or her attitude against intruders. Just as you have protection for credit cards, have locks on your doors, and have a vehicle security system, your attitude needs protection too. Leaders who place high values on their attitudes are more successful than those who don't, mainly because they value others' attitudes too and become good at seeing both sides of a situation.

3. Become a Person One Values as a Friend or Colleague. Since most people enjoy being around happy, energetic people, truly successful leaders are happy, vibrant, energetic people. Leaders value productivity and they respect other people who carry their load. They are good team players and build team spirit. They place a high value on loyalty,

*Elwood N. Chapman and Sharon Lund O'Neil, Your Attitude Is Showing: A Primer of Human Relations, 9th Ed., Upper Saddle River, NJ: Prentice Hall, 1999

honesty, integrity, ethics, and other such values. They practice what they preach. Becoming your own best friend may be a major step toward placing a higher value on yourself. Leaders have found success in this advice.

4. Reduce Tension- and Stress-Inducing Behavior. In general, leaders experience more stress and pressure than managers. They produce stress for themselves by the very nature of the jobs they perform. However, successful leaders have learned that balance in their lives includes good tension releases—walking, manual labor, shopping, reading, etc. What is vital to the leader's good mental health is recognizing what causes tension—in his or her life, as well as in the lives of other people—and employing stress reduction techniques and activities.

5. Take Charge of Your Attitude. A true leader's attitude is real, genuine, and credible. There is no quicker way to lose credibility than to have a phony, superficial demeanor. Leaders cannot afford to lose credibility and will do everything they can to protect it. Leaders know that being in control and taking charge of their own lives *always* produce better results than would be possible with any alternative.

Now, ask yourself how many of these five attitude elements you can identify as your strengths. Can you improve on any of the elements—even though you may feel you "score" high on them? The authors are confident that you can empower your attitude as much as you truly desire toward becoming the leader you aspire to be. Every successful leader knows that her or his positive attitude belongs only to himself or herself— a priceless possession that needs protecting to ensure happiness.

Throughout this book you will be encouraged to compare the traditional concept of a good manager with that of a good leader/manager. Eventually, you will make up your own mind about what the differences are, and you will decide where you want to position yourself.

    If you agree that achieving higher productivity is both a management and a leadership function, the formula postulated in Chapter 3 will have special meaning to you. Before you take your first look at the Model, you are invited to review your leadership potential by completing the following exercise, Leadership Potential Scale.

POSITIONING YOURSELF

LEADERSHIP POTENTIAL SCALE

If you have not had the chance to demonstrate your leadership talents, you may have more potential than you think. This scale is designed to help you evaluate how much potential you possess. Circle the number that best indicates where you fall in the scale. After you have finished, total your scores in the space provided.

	High *Low*	
I can develop the confidence to lead others.	10 9 8 7 6 5 4 3 2 1	I could never develop enough personal confidence to lead.
I could set a strong authority line and make it stick.	10 9 8 7 6 5 4 3 2 1	I could not become an authority figure in any situation.
It would not bother me to discipline those under my leadership.	10 9 8 7 6 5 4 3 2 1	I would find it impossible to discipline someone under my leadership.
I can become an outstanding public speaker.	10 9 8 7 6 5 4 3 2 1	I could never become effective at group communication.
I am confident that I am an excellent decision maker.	10 9 8 7 6 5 4 3 2 1	I do not see myself making decisions that affect others.
I can make hard decisions that would cause others to be upset with me.	10 9 8 7 6 5 4 3 2 1	I don't want anything to do with hard decisions.
It would not bother me to stay aloof from followers.	10 9 8 7 6 5 4 3 2 1	I'd rather be one of the gang.
I am highly self-motivated and seek responsibility.	10 9 8 7 6 5 4 3 2 1	I am not self-motivated; I do not seek responsibility.
I have great compassion for others.	10 9 8 7 6 5 4 3 2 1	I have little or no compassion for others.
I can remain 100 percent positive in a negative environment.	10 9 8 7 6 5 4 3 2 1	I have a difficult time remaining positive in a negative environment.

TOTAL _____

If your score totaled 80 or above, it would appear that you have a very high leadership potential. You have the confidence to be a top-flight leader. If your total was between 60 and 80, you have above-average leadership potential. You will probably do well in many leadership roles. If you scored under 60, you may have underrated yourself or you may simply not be ready for a leadership role at this stage of your life. It is suggested that you complete the scale again after you have finished this book. Keep in mind that the scale is not a scientific instrument; it is nothing more than a self-assessment aid designed to help you measure your potential for development.

* Both management and leadership skills contribute to closing productivity gaps.
* Leaders are recognized as stronger motivators than managers because they inspire their followers.
* Leaders are decisive; they make timely, good decisions.
* Leaders are risk takers who make tough decisions which, in the long run, usually contribute to higher productivity.
* Leaders ask for more responsibility and enjoy making change happen to better position themselves to reach higher productivity levels.
* Leaders drive change; they do not wait for it to happen.
* Leaders have positive attitudes which they protect as prized possessions; they take charge of their attitudes.
* Leaders' positive attitudes contribute to success, especially to good communication.

SUMMARY

Case 3: High Producer?

Gene is an efficient, professional manager. He is a superior planner, always anticipating problems that may appear so he can solve many of them in advance. Gene has an unusually good balance between the technical and the "people" sides of his department, always staying on top of technical advances without neglecting his employees. He is respected by superiors because of his consistent, steady hand and the fact that he has a "trouble free" operation. When Gene's boss does her annual evaluation, she usually says to herself: "Wish we could develop more managers with his capabilities."

Maureen is recognized as an average manager who often shows flashes of leadership. Sometimes, especially during staff meetings, she comes up with ideas that contribute significantly to the organization. Maureen is so goal oriented and sets such a fast pace that employees in other departments talk to each other about how happy they are not to be under her leadership. Management appreciates Maureen, but after her annual performance evaluation, they often say: "Wish she would settle back a little and relax."

Assuming that Gene and Maureen have identical operations within the same organization, which work team would you guess achieves greater productivity?

- ☐ Gene achieves higher productivity.
- ☐ Maureen is the leader in productivity.

Please state in a few words why you selected one over the other and then compare your reasoning with that of the authors (in the back of the book).

_____

_____

_____

Ms. Preston started her career as a teller with a large banking organization twelve years ago. It took her six years to become a branch manager. Today she travels throughout the branch system as an interim manager. Ms. Preston becomes a temporary manager whenever someone resigns or is promoted until a new manager is trained. This usually takes two weeks.

Case 4: Opportunity

Shortly after she started this rescue procedure (three years ago), some astounding things happened. Customer complaints would decrease, as would employee absenteeism, and deposits would increase. Management decided that Ms. Preston had a way of pulling a branch together in a short time and training a new manager in such a way that improvements continued. She always left each assignment with a party in her honor!

Yesterday the bank management met to fill the newly created position of Director of Human Resources. Although everyone expected the personnel director to be promoted into the position, the chairperson suggested that Ms. Preston be given the job. "She is obviously one of the best leaders around here, she knows the branch operations better than the personnel director, and she achieves productivity quickly."

The director of branch operations (on the management team) replied: "I agree with everything you say, but I think her contribution is greater where she is now. I suggest we give her a raise, have her spend even more time training new managers, and have her teach a leadership training seminar here at headquarters on a continuing basis. In this way, her productivity contribution will be greater. As a strong leader, she belongs in operations and not in a staff position."

If you were on the company board, whom would you support? Why? State your case below and compare it to the authors' views (in the back of the book).

Self-Test   Mark each statement True (T) or False (F).

_____ 1. The primary goal of management is higher productivity.

_____ 2. In the same situation, a leader/manager can often create higher productivity than a manager.

_____ 3. Most managers ask for more responsibility.

_____ 4. Most leaders believe that change, even without direction or a plan, is positive.

_____ 5. Most managers are risk takers.

_____ 6. Managers are known for their ability to develop employees into followers.

_____ 7. Productivity can fall after a tough "people decision," but increase to a higher level within a short time.

_____ 8. Most leaders have positive attitudes which enhance their overall abilities.

_____ 9. Good communication skills are frequently the key to getting a goal accomplished.

_____10. There is always a slight gap between what an organization produces and what it is capable of producing.

Turn to the back of the book to check your answers.

TOTAL CORRECT _____

3 Adopt the Leadership Formula (Leadership Strategic Model)

A person does not become a leader by virtue of the possession of some combination of traits.

Ralph Stogdill

3 Adopt the Leadership Formula (Leadership Strategic Model)

In this chapter you will be introduced the Leadership Formula, or prescription, for increasing your leadership potential. The Leadership Formula is really a strategic model for you to follow in acquiring the successful skills, techniques, and principles that are commonly practiced by men and women who occupy leadership roles in a variety of settings. The Formula was not developed merely from reading and observation, but was derived and synthesized from the results of interviews with numerous successful leaders in business, education, sports, religion, youth organizations, politics, and community groups.

The Leadership Formula is as follows:

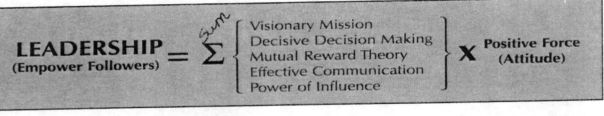

$$\text{LEADERSHIP (Empower Followers)} = \sum_{} \begin{cases} \text{Visionary Mission} \\ \text{Decisive Decision Making} \\ \text{Mutual Reward Theory} \\ \text{Effective Communication} \\ \text{Power of Influence} \end{cases} \times \text{Positive Force (Attitude)}$$

where "Leadership" is based on the ability to "Empower Followers" and equals the sum of five critical elements or factors ("Visionary Mission," "Decisive Decision Making," "Mutual Reward Theory," "Effective Communication," and "Power of Influence") times a sixth element, "Positive Force," which is based on your attitude.

Said another way, leadership involves maximizing each of six factors. And what is critical to the Formula's success is keeping your attitude as positive as possible to maximize each of the elements.

Your success in applying the Leadership Formula depends on the degree of mastery you can attain in of each of the six elements represented in the equation. To explain the Leadership Formula, let's look at a graphic illustration of the Formula—the Leadership Strategic Model. In the graphic, the Leadership Formula becomes a star with five points. Each of the five points represents a fundamental premise of leadership; the center (nucleus) of the star represents the sixth factor:

1. Visionary Mission—the ability to see the big picture and to formulate a plan of action to reach a lofty goal.

2. Decisive Decision Making—the ability to delegate effectively and make good, timely decisions.

LEADERSHIP STRATEGIC MODEL

VISIONARY
MISSION

POWER
OF INFLUENCE

DECISIVE
DECISION
MAKING

POSITIVE
FORCE
(ATTITUDE)

EFFECTIVE
COMMUNICATION

MUTUAL
REWARD
THEORY

EMPOWERED FOLLOWERS

3. Mutual Reward Theory—the ability to enhance relationships based on a balance of rewards for all people involved.

4. Effective Communication—the ability to convey meaning (through writing, speaking, and non-verbal actions) for understanding.

5. Power of Influence—the ability to persuade others toward desired actions.

6. Positive Force—the ability to motivate and stimulate others to take action.

The positive force as the center of the star really is a person's positive attitude. It is attitude—that positive force—that maximizes each of the other elements. Attitude is the self-igniting spark, the positive force, that extends energy to the outer points (elements) of the star.

From Chapter 2 you have learned that your attitude is your most priceless possession. Attitude is also the driving force which propels you into action. As each of the five elements of the Leadership Model is discussed in the chapters to follow, pay particular attention to the importance that continues to be placed on attitude. Your positive attitude is a key component in how successful you will be in developing your leadership skills.

Finally, note that the star is firmly anchored to a foundation—empowered followers. Empowered followers result from good leadership. We cannot forget that the franchise to lead comes from followers, not from superiors, nor from organizations.

LEADERSHIP ELEMENTS ARE INTERRELATED

The Leadership Formula, when transformed into the graphic, becomes the Leadership Strategic Model. The Model is the key to building your leadership skills. While each of the elements of the Leadership Strategic Model will be discussed in detail in later chapters, one final point is important here. That is, all of the elements or fundamentals that make up the Leadership Formula are interrelated, interlocked, and interdependent.

For example, without EFFECTIVE COMMUNICATION from the leader, it would be impossible to create and maintain a motivating VISIONARY MISSION. It would also be extremely difficult to engage in DECISIVE DECISION MAKING. Similarly, without practicing the MUTUAL REWARD THEORY, relationships with followers could not be built, let alone be maximized to empower them to create a powerful team. Additionally, any single one of the other elements cannot contribute significantly to successful leadership without utilizing the POWER of INFLUENCE. Finally, it follows that POSITIVE FORCE (based on a positive attitude) is the driving power to fully mobilize the other five elements.

The importance of the Leadership Strategic Model cannot be over-estimated. You may want to refer to the graphic model occasionally as you learn more about each of the "star's" elements for effective leadership development.

However, let's turn now to some of the questions and answers that form the basis for the Leadership Formula.

Some important questions were explored by those who helped develop the Formula as well as by others who have used the Formula with various leaders and potential leaders. Because you may have the same concerns, we have included several of the most important questions here:

PRELIMINARY QUESTIONS AND ANSWERS

> **Question 1: Will the Leadership Formula accommodate different management styles?**

Yes. The object of the Leadership Strategic Model (Leadership Formula) is to put more leadership into your present style, not to change it. A manager who is comfortable with a strong approach can adjust the Formula to fit his or her style. So can an individual who believes in and practices participative management.

Some people have a strong human relations orientation in their style; others are more task oriented. Some "practice" a leadership style or behavior that is very direct (tell people what to do and closely monitor or supervise progress); others exercise their leadership in a more supportive or facilitating role (a coaching style that promotes listening to suggestions while moving toward task accomplishment). And some lean more heavily on their personalities than others. It is not necessary to discard your basic style to adopt the Formula. It will fit into all comfort zones.

> **Question 2: Will adopting the Formula improve my management style?**

Definitely. Any move you make to strengthen your leadership will also strengthen your management style, provided one is not neglected for the other. The Formula will add substance to most management styles, no matter what their stage of development. Through adoption of the Formula, you are in a position to see weak areas in your management style not previously noticed. In some cases, a new thrust in leadership development will strengthen the weak areas in management.

> **Question 3: Does my career future depends on discovering just the right blend of management and leadership?**

If you wish to accept the challenge leadership offers, the answer is yes. Once achieved, it doesn't matter whether you refer to the results as your management or your leadership style. Inevitably, it is a combination of both.

> **Question 4: Why isn't integrity a part of the Leadership Formula?**

Integrity, like compassion, tolerance, and fairness, is a personal trait, standard, or characteristic. Although integrity is of ultimate significance on moral grounds, the Leadership Formula does not differentiate. The authors strongly recommend that integrity and ethics become integral to your leadership style. However, we can identify many leaders that may have varying degrees of integrity. And keep in mind that both Gandhi and Hitler were powerful leaders.

> **Question 5: Will one weak point diminish the strength of the star?**

Although one cannot expect to develop equal strength in all of the elements of the Leadership Formula, a severe weakness in one of the factors can cause other points to lose their luster. That is, you should strive to reach as high a level as possible, developing to the fullest each of the elements of the Formula. Reaching a good balance in your leadership development—just as in life—is always a good rule to follow.

SYMBOLISM OF THE STAR

> **Question 6: What is the symbolism of the star?**

Whatever you wish it to be. Some people feel the star represents a person who excels; others see it as a symbol of authority; still others view leadership in any environment as a "star" role. A few like to interpret it as a visionary symbol that causes followers to follow.

Question 7: Some authors use a situational approach to leadership. They seem to say that each environment requires a different kind of leader. Are they wrong?

No. Different situations require different approaches, understandings, sensitivities, and styles. The great advantage to the Leadership Strategic Model is that it has distilled those basics common to and necessary for success in all situations. It can, therefore, apply as well to a military officer as a politician, a coach or a corporate officer, a minister or a community leader. If a leader moves from one environment to another, certain adjustments to style should be made; once the Formula foundations have been mastered, they can be applied to each new situation.

Question 8: Will the Leadership Formula benefit experienced leaders as well as beginners?

LEADERS CAN IMPROVE THEIR LEADERSHIP

Yes. The difference could be that successful leaders might be content to use the Formula to identify one or more weak areas in their style of leadership, whereas beginners might wish to build their complete style around the Formula.

Question 9: Is the Leadership Formula designed for business leaders only?

Absolutely not. The Formula will make sense to those who occupy or hope to occupy any leadership role—everything from a student leader in high school to the President of the United States. The Formula does, however, incorporate good management practices.

Question 10: Will the Formula help produce a better kind of leader for the future?

Yes, because all bases are covered: nothing is left to chance. Properly interpreted and employed, the Leadership Strategic Model can produce a stronger, more decisive leader and one who is, at the same time, more sensitive to the real needs of followers. Strong, decisive leaders who are sensitive to people's needs are the kind of leaders that are desperately needed at all levels of our society.

LEADERS EMPOWER FOLLOWERS

Question 11: What kind of followers do leaders desire?

Successful and enduring leaders want their followers to be knowledgeable and fully informed on all aspects of an operation. As a result, they strive for openness and avoid giving any hint of undercover or secret activities. Leaders do whatever is necessary to clarify misunderstandings quickly and promote open, two-way communication. Leaders recognize that their future depends on enlightened followers. They know that distrust quickly destroys their opportunity to lead.

The most successful leaders empower their followers. That is, the stronger each follower is, the more each can do. The better decision maker each follower is, the easier it is to push the bigger decisions down to lower levels. And if followers are sensitive to human relations, it is less likely that the leader will need to get too involved with time-consuming people conflicts.

Question 12: Do leaders train leaders beneath them?

Some leaders, but not all, train key staff members on the fundamentals of leadership. They recognize that the more leaders they have following them, the better. And they seek two special characteristics in these follower-leaders:

1. individuals who will speak up and, when justified, take opposing views;

2. individuals who develop their own leadership style internally, but reflect the leader's style externally for image purposes. Overconformity that creates blind followership is to be avoided at all costs.

ADOPT THE LEADERSHIP FORMULA AS YOUR OWN

As you proceed in developing your leadership skills and style, keep in mind that the essence of leadership cannot be defined in a sentence or paragraph. Rather, it is to be found in all the principles presented in the book. Use the Leadership Formula (Leadership Strategic Model) to guide you. Challenge yourself to adopt the Leadership Formula as your own—and put more leadership in your style.

SUMMARY

*   Most people who want to become successful leaders possess a combination of other traits and skills that make it possible.
*   The Leadership Formula can be expressed (illustrated by a star) as the Leadership Strategic Model.
*   The Leadership Strategic Model is a practical road map designed to help people at all levels to weave more of the leadership elements into their styles.
*   The Leadership Formula describes leadership as based on the ability to empower followers via six major elements: visionary mission, decisive decision making, mutual reward theory, effective communication, power of influence, and positive force (attitude).
*   A positive attitude is central to the Leadership Formula; it is a vital element in the development of your leadership ability.
*   The Leadership Formula, as illustrated by the Leadership Strategic Model, is a composite of successful practices used by leaders in a wide variety of roles.

As noted earlier, each of the elements and fundamentals of the Leadership Strategic Model (Leadership Formula) are explained more fully in the following chapters of the book.

Case 5: Conflict

Greg and Vicki are enrolled in an evening leadership course offered by the graduate school of the university. Although the course provides credit toward an MBA, students from other disciplines and community leaders are welcome. During the evening break, Greg and Vicki get into a friendly discussion. They are both excited about that night's lecture—on leadership.

"I am convinced," states Greg, "that leadership must be analyzed and understood from a purely situational point of view. Start with the environment and then build a model. The military requires one kind of leader, business another, and other environments still others. The situation dictates the substance as well as the style. I have had nothing but trouble trying to use my military leadership skills in business. I'm having to start from scratch."

"This is hard for me to accept, Greg," replied Vicki. "If what you say is true, then people must wait until they get into a specific environment before building up leadership skills. To me, leadership is leadership. If you learn the essentials in one situation, you can take them with you to another. If you are a general in the army, you can take your leadership capabilities with you into politics. Eisenhower did this. If you are a recognized leader in business, you can take your basic skills with you into government or education. The real basics or substance of leadership are the same in all environments. Only minor adjustments need to be made to fit the situation, and most of those should be in approach and style. Maybe you learned techniques instead of fundamentals in the military, and that is why you are having trouble adjusting them to your new environment."

Whom would you support—Greg or Vicki? Why? (The authors' opinions are given in the back of the book.)

Bob Stark, a candidate for city council position in the 5th district, was talking with his campaign manager, Joan Burke, about his campaign strategy. The discussion turned to leadership.

Case 6: Potential

"Joan, I agree that leadership is the key to any politician's success, but I also believe that leadership evolves in a natural way and deliberate attempts at improvement might backfire. My present style is working, so I'm reluctant to add any new components. All it needs is a little polishing. Why tinker with success?"

"I totally disagree, Bob. Polishing your style is good, but there may be some fundamentals of leadership that you have yet to incorporate into your style. Adding just one of them could make a major difference to your political future. I believe that most politicians operate far beneath their leadership potential. They have blind spots in their style. And they keep on making the same old mistakes, trusting that image and exposure will keep them in office."

"Well, Joan, if you feel that my leadership skills need sharpening, then I suppose I could study others and adopt what I like into my style. But nobody can distill the basics of leadership. Nobody can say these are the essentials and these are not. Leadership is not an absolute."

"Sorry, Bob, but there must be a few fundamentals that belong in any style. And you may be jeopardizing your political career because of your tunnel vision."

Do you agree with Bob or Joan? Support your view. (The authors' views are given in the back of the book.)

Self-Test

Mark each statement True (T) or False (F).

_____ 1. Your leadership potential can be increased if you work at acquiring certain common skills, techniques, and principles.

_____ 2. The Leadership Formula or Leadership Strategic Model emphasizes six critical elements that are vital to empower followers.

_____ 3. The Leadership Formula postulates that your positive attitude is the key component in how successful you will be in developing your leadership skills.

_____ 4. The directive vs. the supportive type of leader is always more successful because he or she can more readily get tasks accomplished.

_____ 5. The elements of the Leadership Strategic Model are interrelated; that is, the success of one factor frequently depends on another.

_____ 6. The Leadership Formula will accommodate all basic leadership styles.

_____ 7. Communication is not a part of the Leadership Formula.

_____ 8. Empowered followers result from good leadership.

_____ 9. The Leadership Formula is designed to add substance to style.

_____10. The essence of leadership is the Formula or Model itself.

Turn to the back of the book to check your answers.

TOTAL CORRECT _____

4 Be an Effective Communicator

Communication is something so simple and difficult that we can never put it in simple words.

T.S. Mathews

4 Be an Effective Communicator

LEADERS OUTSHINE MANAGERS AS COMMUNICATORS

As managers move into leadership roles, they go through a transition that can be rather dramatic. In no other area is this transitional change more pronounced than in communication. Professional seminar leaders, many classroom instructors and trainers and sports coaches, to name a few, know the importance of developing good communication skills—writing, speaking, listening, nonverbal gesturing, etc.

Skill development training—in communication, human relations (including attitude), and other "soft" skill areas—has become an integral part of an increasing number of training programs. And the emphasis on communication skills has seen phenomenal expansion in recent years. At the college level, for example, students can now pursue full degrees in several specialities within the communication discipline. Many other degree programs are requiring general as well as specialty communication courses. The reason for the increased focus on communication is simple: human relations—with communication skills as a central component—is still the most important factor in the hiring and firing of employees.

Before we enter into a further discussion of communication and related elements, ask yourself how you rate as a communicator. The Leadership Communication Scale that follows will help you assess your present communication skills.

An excellent way to be more objective about your communication skills—in addition to rating yourself on the Scale—is to have another person rate you on the same Scale, and then compare the two scores. (Note that two forms of the Scale are provided—one for you and one for an evaluator.) The person you select to rate you should be concerned about your future (a close friend, family member, or close associate/supervisor). Your evaluator should be in a position to observe your communication skills. Your evaluator also should be someone who will be open with you—not someone who will give you only high ratings because she or he does not want to hurt your feelings.

Further, **YOU** must be open minded and accept the "frankness" of your evaluator as his or her assessment of what she or he *perceives* is your present communication skills level. For a more accurate picture of how others perceive you, you may want to ask several people to rate you on the Leadership Communication Scale. Where there is strong agreement among frank evaluators, you can be fairly confident of the way your communication effectiveness is viewed by others.

LEADERSHIP COMMUNICATION SCALE
(Form for You to Rate Your Skills)

Circle the number that best indicates where you fall in the scale, and enter the total in the space at the bottom.

	High ⟶ Low	
I am constantly aware of my communication responsibilities.	10 9 8 7 6 5 4 3 2 1	I need to be reminded over and over about the importance of communication.
I understand fully the importance of nonverbal communication. I always project an outstanding visual image.	10 9 8 7 6 5 4 3 2 1	I constantly need to be reminded that there is such a thing as nonverbal communication. People must accept me the way I am.
I have learned how to keep my audience's attention when I talk to any size group.	10 9 8 7 6 5 4 3 2 1	The moment I start to talk, I sense people are taking their minds elsewhere.
Rate me a "10" as a listener. I have developed all the skills and I practice them.	10 9 8 7 6 5 4 3 2 1	Give me a "1." I am a terrible listener.
I know how to adjust my conversation to the vocabulary and interest levels of others.	10 9 8 7 6 5 4 3 2 1	I always seem to be talking to myself.
I use appropriate voice control, diction, and delivery techniques.	10 9 8 7 6 5 4 3 2 1	I've given up on becoming an average presenter/speaker.
I seem to be able to pick just the right words to convey my message.	10 9 8 7 6 5 4 3 2 1	I'm clumsy with words. I'm always putting my foot in my mouth.
My written, spoken, and nonverbal messages are clear, concise, and well received.	10 9 8 7 6 5 4 3 2 1	If I get any feedback at all, it is bad.
I never over- or undertalk. I'm always on target.	10 9 8 7 6 5 4 3 2 1	I either say too much or too little.
I instinctively know which media to use, and I fully employ all communication systems available.	10 9 8 7 6 5 4 3 2 1	Not only do I fail to use the right media, I do not take advantage of the opportunities available.

TOTAL _____

If you rated yourself 80 or above, you appear to possess outstanding communication skills. If you rated yourself between 60 and 80, you may be getting a signal that some improvement is necessary if you are to reach your leadership potential. If you rated yourself under 60, it would appear that substantial improvement is needed.

LEADERSHIP COMMUNICATION SCALE
(Form for Another Person to Rate Your Skills)

Evaluatee_____ Evaluator_____

Circle the number that best indicates where the evaluatee falls in the scale, and enter the total in the space at the bottom.

	High 10 9 8 7 6 5 4 3 2 1 *Low*	
Is constantly aware of his/her communication responsibilities.	10 9 8 7 6 5 4 3 2 1	Needs to be reminded over and over about the importance of communication.
Fully understands the importance of nonverbal communication. Always projects an outstanding visual image.	10 9 8 7 6 5 4 3 2 1	Constantly needs to be reminded that there is such a thing as nonverbal communication. People must accept him/her the way he/she is.
Has learned how to keep an audience's attention when he/she talks to any size group.	10 9 8 7 6 5 4 3 2 1	The moment he/she starts to talk, there is the sense that people are taking their minds elsewhere.
Rates a "10" as a listener. Has developed all the skills and practices them.	10 9 8 7 6 5 4 3 2 1	Give her/him a "1." He/she is a terrible listener.
Knows how to adjust his/her conversation to the vocabulary and interest levels of others.	10 9 8 7 6 5 4 3 2 1	Always seems to be talking to her/himself.
Uses appropriate voice control, diction, and delivery techniques.	10 9 8 7 6 5 4 3 2 1	Has given up on becoming an average presenter/speaker.
Seems to be able to pick just the right words to convey her/his message.	10 9 8 7 6 5 4 3 2 1	Is clumsy with words. Is always putting his/her foot in mouth.
Written, spoken, and nonverbal messages are clear, concise, and well received.	10 9 8 7 6 5 4 3 2 1	If he/she gets any feedback at all, it is bad.
Never over- or undertalks. Is always on target.	10 9 8 7 6 5 4 3 2 1	Either says too much or too little.
Instinctively knows which media to use, and fully employs all communication systems available.	10 9 8 7 6 5 4 3 2 1	Not only does he/she fail to use the right media, he/she does not take advantage of the opportunities available.

TOTAL _____

If you were rated 80 or above, you appear (to other people in the eyes of your evaluator) to possess outstanding communication skills. If you were rated between 60 and 80, you may be getting a signal that some improvement is necessary if you are to reach your leadership potential. If you were rated under 60, it would appear that substantial improvement is needed.

As the leadership rating exercise demonstrates, communication is much more than being an excellent writer or speaker. Good communication involves understanding people (and their styles), being informed, thinking and making value judgments, conducting and participating in meetings, contributing to goals and teams, keeping others informed, understanding informal transmission modes (the grapevine, rumormill, etc.), sending nonverbal messages, listening, and staying positive.

Leaders must be good communicators because they have a considerable amount of responsibility for assuring good communication among team members. Teamwork is extremely dependent upon successful communication. Thus, good communication is a vital element for team success—and for "teams" well beyond those in the workplace, including family, friendships, sports, etc.—and will help you in all aspects of your life.

The remainder of the chapter will focus on ways you can expand your ability to become a skillful communicator. Keep in mind that communication is an essential component of the Leadership Formula or Leadership Strategic Model (Chapter 3); thus, communication is, without a doubt, a skill you need for leadership success.

LEADERS KNOW HOW TO USE THEIR NONVERBAL SKILLS

Nonverbal gesturing is one of the most important communication skills a leader can possess. You, of course, have heard the saying, "actions speak louder than words". Believe it! A leader can have eloquent speech, be professionally dressed, and be talented in many others ways only to "lose out" because of his or her lack of good *nonverbal* skills.

Nonverbal skills refer to your body language or "signals." That is, you give off positive or negative signals with your facial expression (bright eyes, smile, and interested look on your face); your voice (positive, neither monotone nor gruff, upbeat inflection, good diction and enunciation, and even choice of words—avoiding slang or talking down to people, etc.); your stance (showing confidence without being cocky, good posture, leaning forward in your chair, legs uncrossed and "pointed" in the direction of your audience, etc.); and your "openness" (unfolding arms, avoiding interlocking fingers, forming a triangle with your hands or arms indicating you are willing to listen).

Body language is one of those important characteristics that can make or break you. Leaders know that their most important asset is a positive attitude. And body language or nonverbal gesturing is the main conveyer of a positive attitude—especially when you are speaking and listening.

LEADERS MUST BE SUPERIOR LISTENERS

Good communicators have little "radar" sets, so to speak, that are constantly tuned into others, seeing and understanding others' needs as well as observing how they respond to day-to-day situations. While both lead-

Of course I'm listening!

ers and followers benefit from having this "radar" skill, communication radar is absolutely essential for leaders.

Most people know when they are being listened to and when they are being tuned out. Leaders will not remain leaders very long if they cannot get their followers and teams to listen to them. Similarly, when followers no longer believe their leader hears them, they start looking for a new leader. Sometimes the new leader is a fellow employee who "emerges"—a person who is willing to listen. In this case, the new leader has been informally appointed.

Informal leadership frequently emerges from comments such as these:

"I don't think my leader is as good at listening as she thinks she is."
"I have, when possible, walked away from leaders who failed to consult me."
"Leaders unseat themselves when they make the mistake of listening to a few close followers and ignoring the rest of us."

An informal leader usually is a co-worker who does not have a company leadership position unlike the formal leader who has a designated leadership title. Informal leaders can significantly help (or hinder) a work team depending on a) how supportive they are of the organization's goals, b) how supportive they are toward management or the formal team leader, and c) how they interact with co-workers and other employees, leaders, and teams in the organization.

Listening, then, is a vital communication skill, especially for leaders. Ask yourself the following questions about your listening skills:

MY LISTENING SKILLS		
	Yes	*No*
Do I "show" people I am listening to them (and not thinking about something else—such as what I plan to say next)?	☐	☐
Do I allow subordinates to express their thoughts without interruptions?	☐	☐
Do I know what my followers (or friends) are really thinking?	☐	☐
Do I have a reputation among my colleagues as a good listener?	☐	☐

In your quest to become a better leader, write in the box below the percentage of improvement you would like to achieve in your listening skills.

| % |

Good leaders know when to be quiet listeners. They also know when to be engaging conversationalists. They know how to start informal, one-on-one conversations in any environment. They are experts at dissipating psychological barriers between themselves and their followers. They are perceptive in the questions they ask; they are skilled in the way they ask them.

For example, if you listen carefully to a skillful communicator who is discussing a problem with a group, you will frequently hear the leader refer to the problem as an area of concern, an issue, a challenge, etc., rather than as a "problem." Consider for a moment your receptiveness to a problem presented as a concern, issue, or challenge. Are you more receptive to the latter terms? If so, you also will be more positive and willing to join in the discussion.

It takes only a few moments for a good leader to introduce an important subject, communicate a goal, and reinforce a relationship with a subordinate who may have been neglected or who may have been headed in the wrong direction. A good leader has a way of gaining attention, conveying a message, and leaving a subordinate with the sense that he or she had been a full partner in the dialogue. Thus, when successful leaders circulate among employees within the organization, they leave a wake of newly challenged followers behind them.

A leader's function, in assisting employees to become empowered employees, frequently takes on the role of a counselor. A leader's counseling hat is a difficult one to wear. It requires a very delicate balance of what to do, when to do it, how it should be done (strategy or technique), and with whom (the essential players—frequently a one-on-one situation if a delicate issue needs attention). When successful leaders work with or counsel their subordinates, they practice the 5 R's of communication.

LEADERS MUST BE EXPERTS AT ONE-ON-ONE COMMUNICATION

RIGHT PURPOSE:	They counsel only when there is high probability it will improve the leader-follower or co-worker relationship.
RIGHT TIMING:	They counsel when the mood on both sides appears appropriate and as soon as possible after the issue has arisen.
RIGHT PLACE:	They select private locations where there will be few interruptions and the subordinate's privacy is protected.
RIGHT APPROACH:	They are nonthreatening in their approach and are receptive to the other person's feelings and needs.
RIGHT TECHNIQUE:	When it is necessary to discipline followers, they also inspire them to improve.

Ask yourself the following questions about your one-on-one communication skills.

MY ONE-ON-ONE COMMUNICATION SKILLS

	Yes	No
Do people enjoy private conversations with me to the point that they seek me out?	☐	☐
Can I quickly establish a nonthreatening conversational climate with a subordinate?	☐	☐
Can I give followers the impression they have done 50 percent of the talking even if they have not?	☐	☐
Can I, through a private conversation, convert a disenchanted employee into a empowered follower?	☐	☐

Write in the box below the percentage of improvement you would like to see in your one-on-one communication.

%

LEADERS MUST FACILITATE SMALL-GROUP DYNAMICS

Dr. Lockwood's colleagues could not figure why her students were so enthusiastic about her seminars at the university. Was it her youth and style? Her command of her subject? If asked, Dr. Lockwood's students would have talked about her touch in working with small groups—her ability to draw a reluctant student into a discussion, her skill at turning a hostile student's response into a statement the group could consider in a positive way, and her competency at sensing and articulating the meaning and mood of group discussions. Most of all, they would have mentioned how she used just the right amount of leadership to keep the group on track without stifling creativity.

A leader must be tuned into the dynamics of small groups and be able to facilitate the many aspects of group processes. He or she must know how to facilitate consensus and at the same time improve relationships with all those involved. Balancing group dynamics is not an easy task. Still, a leader who cannot function well in a small-group setting is severely handicapped.

Evaluate your own small-group communication skills with these questions.

MY SMALL-GROUP FACILITATION SKILLS

	Yes	No
Am I relaxed, comfortable, and effective when leading a small-group or team discussion?	☐	☐
Can I perceive and communicate group thinking patterns back to the members, for the best decision to be made?	☐	☐
Can I redirect a complacent group in the right direction, without discouraging contributions from one or more members?	☐	☐
Can I get all group members to contribute something to a discussion?	☐	☐

What percentage of improvement would you like to see in your small-group communication skills?

%

Most leaders seek advice from a few select, competent individuals on their staffs—people they can depend on for loyalty, competency, a broad perspective, and just plain good advice. It should be rather obvious, then, why staff selection is very critical to a leader's success. Many people have lost their opportunities to lead because they failed to surround themselves with the best advisors. Leaders who operate in a vacuum will not remain in leadership roles very long.

LEADERS SURROUND THEMSELVES WITH STRONG STAFF

Successful leaders have the capacity to develop an inner circle of staff people who are loyal and competent. A strong staff is especially important when the leader has a large span of control (span of control is the total number of employees for whom the leader or manager is responsible).

Good communication skills help to create and maintain the close bond between a leader and his or her staff. Staff meetings should create an *espirt de corps*—a spirit that encourages loyalty and avoids dissension. Also, staff meetings should provide everyone with the opportunity to speak on all issues. And each staff meeting should contribute to the improvement of vertical relationships (between the leader and her or his staff) as well as of horizontal relationships (among staff members). Most importantly, participants should feel there was some value in the meeting, such as progress toward a goal or clarification of a point, process, or misunderstanding.

A good leader's staff becomes an extension of his or her image or leadership style. The staff's extension of the leader's style does not mean that everyone must become an image of the leader. It means that each staff member, in her or his own way, contributes to the leader's style. In turn, as the leader increases her or his effectiveness through a competent staff, the leader's overall impact is enhanced.

Some experts give staff selection top priority, but it is not only selection that counts. Leaders know that the development of good relationships with all individuals through group communication is an important rule to follow. All highly successful leaders—coaches, ministers, community leaders, corporate executives, and politicians—eventually become small-group communication experts. Many leaders take special seminars early in their development, as well as periodically, to enhance these skills.

LEADERS MUST BECOME SUPERIOR SPEAKERS/ PRESENTERS

All leaders take advantage of opportunities to present to large groups. Some are inspirational, and their leadership image is greatly enhanced. Some are moderately inspirational, and their image is protected. Those who are credible (but noninspirational) speakers need to compensate by improving their image in other areas. Positive body language, or using good nonverbal skills, is an excellent way to create a positive reaction from an audience.

When it comes to leadership, becoming an outstanding speaker is a major advantage. If you work on making your attitude as positive as you can, you will have more confidence in making presentations to large groups. A positive attitude also is easily detected by audiences. Remember, *Your Attitude Is Showing** in everything you do!

Answer these questions about your presentation skills.

MY LARGE-GROUP PRESENTATION SKILLS

	Yes	No
Do I show confidence and a positive attitude when I speak to large audiences?	☐	☐
Am I good at audience analysis to determine how I am being perceived?	☐	☐
Am I skillful at receiving, interpreting, and answering difficult questions in large groups?	☐	☐
After speaking to a large group, do I feel good about myself and my presentation skills?	☐	☐

Write the percentage of improvement you would like to see in your large-group presentation/speaking skills.

| % |

---

*Elwood N. Chapman and Sharon Lund O'Neil, Your Attitude is Showing: A Primer of Human Relations, 9th Ed., Upper Saddle River, NJ: Prentice Hall, 1999.

Few leaders are in a position to employ professional ghost writers (although some may hide behind the skills of gifted assistants). Most must rely on their own competencies. They must—word by word, sentence by sentence—write their own letters, bulletins, and memos to people inside and outside the organization. They must prepare their own presentations. They must make sure their written messages will grab the reader's (or listener's) attention, carry the message they wish to convey, not be misinterpreted, and be free from errors.

LEADERS DO NOT NEGLECT THEIR WRITING SKILLS

Subordinates want their leader's messages to reflect his or her leadership style. They want powerful and decisive messages. Otherwise, the absence of the leader's stamp is quickly noted.

The following questions will help you evaluate your writing skills.

MY WRITING SKILLS

	Yes	No
Am I proud of my writing skills?	☐	☐
Do I use my writing skills effectively, avoid jargon, meet my audience at their level, and command attention and response?	☐	☐
Do I send written messages even though it is easier, but not as effective, to use the telephone?	☐	☐
Do I write my own messages rather than depend on others to protect my leadership image?	☐	☐

Write the percentage of improvement you would like to show in your written communication.

%

Two-way information and communication networks are more critical to leaders than to managers because leaders are more vulnerable to disenchanted followers and competitive factions. Thus, to protect themselves, leaders need advance information that only a good communication system can provide about problem situations.

LEADERS CREATE AND MAINTAIN A COMMUNICATION NETWORK

Just as most sports teams employ talent scouts, leaders need people they can trust to keep them informed about all phases of their operation. In an efficient network, this data can come from three primary sources:

1. Inside Follower Contacts. No matter how large the organization, a leader needs feedback from followers at all levels, especially those

at the bottom of the hierarchy. This may mean frequent visits and informal interviews with various departments or branches. One-on-one counseling can be a gold mine for finding out how followers really feel.

2. Outside Professional Contacts. Most leaders are not satisfied to depend exclusively on inside contacts. They know that insiders are not privy to knowledge that outsiders have about an organization. Also, outsiders view things differently than insiders. That is why professional consultants often play a key role in many aspects of furthering a company's goals.

3. Staff Information Magnets. Some staff members are better as reliable information providers than others. These individuals should be encouraged, protected, and complimented. At the same time, favoritism should not be shown. Also, a leader should guard against overdependence on one source and the possibility that jealousies might be generated.

Although one goal of a communication system is to identify problems ahead of time so that solutions can be reached before major conflicts arise, a much larger goal is a steady flow of accurate data for decision making.

For managers to be star leaders, they must learn to be effective communicators. They must be alert listeners, good counselors and staff leaders, excellent speakers and presenters, good writers, and sensitive nonverbal communicators. In addition, they also must have positive attitudes, understand people, develop good overall human relationships (vertically and horizontally), and devise a networking system to fit their organization and their personality.

The leader's job is a big one! And, the easiest way to lose one's license to lead is to neglect followers or neglect empowering them.

SUMMARY

* To become a successful leader, one must excel at many forms of communication including: listening, counseling, speaking and presenting, writing, nonverbal gesturing, etc.
* Leaders who understand people and the dynamics of a small group can facilitate productive staff meetings.
* Through sensitive one-on-one conversations, leaders can develop reluctant followers into empowered followers.
* Leaders greatly enhance their image when they become stars at speaking and presenting to all sizes and types of groups.

* To keep informed for good decision making, leaders need staff advisors, professional contacts, and an efficient, two-way networking system.

* Failure to become superior communicators leaves many managers behind in the leadership race.

Case 7: Improvement   Katina Blake has, for some time, been debating in her mind whether to strengthen her communication skills by taking a course in presentation skills. She has been told by close friends that although she has natural ability as a speaker, she should take a course to sharpen her skills. But every time a course is offered, Katina backs away from making a decision. She rationalizes that she can become a better presenter without formal help.

Yesterday she was invited to speak to over five hundred people at a convention next spring. She accepted, knowing it would be her biggest, most important audience ever. The talk will be critical to her leadership image. In making her plans, she decides she has three possibilities for improving her presentation skills:

1. Use video tape to improve her speaking ability on a do-it-yourself basis.

2. Take a course in public speaking or professional communication. Ample time remains.

3. Rely on her natural ability, but get more experience in front of groups of all sizes before the big day arrives.

Which of the above strategies do you feel would provide Ms. Blake with the most help? Second? Third? If you were in her shoes, what additional experiences would you seek? (The authors' rankings are given in the back of the book.)

Celine and Matthew, both in their mid-thirties, have attained middle-management positions with a large utility. Although there has been considerable downsizing in the firm recently, both feel secure in their positions and can see opportunities for further growth.

Yesterday, after working later than usual, Celine and Matthew decided to let the heavy downtown traffic dissipate before going home, and their conversation turned in the direction of career progress.

"Celine," said Matthew, "so far our progress has been similar, but from now on I think it is a new ball game. Our future will depend as much on our leadership as on our management ability."

"I agree," replied Celine. "That is why I have decided to go back to the university and get a master's degree in communication. I think it is the best way to put more leadership into my management style. What do you think?"

"I think it would be a mistake. What you really need is a masters in business administration. At least that is going to be my ticket."

"MBAs are a dime a dozen around here. Becoming a superior platform speaker and all-around communicator will enhance my leadership ability better than more management training. You want an MBA for status purposes more than for what it will do for your capacity to lead."

Would you defend Celine or Matthew?

Earning an MBA will contribute to Matthew's management and leadership ability. It is his best bet.   ☐

Celine has the right idea. Communication training will do more for her leadership skill than a higher degree in management.   ☐

(The authors' comments are given in the back of the book.)

Self-Test

Mark each statement True (T) or False (F).

_____ 1. To demonstrate leadership, managers should be better at all phases of communication than their followers.

_____ 2. For both leaders and managers, speaking is always more important than nonverbal communication.

_____ 3. Would-be leaders should start delegating as many writing responsibilities as possible while they are managers.

_____ 4. Followers want to be inspired by their leaders; platform speaking provides an excellent way for leaders to do this.

_____ 5. Communication is an absolutely essential component of the Leadership Formula or Leadership Strategic Model.

_____ 6. A person who scores below 60 on the Leadership Communication Scale could never be a leader.

_____ 7. Leaders who are poor listeners often lose their followers without knowing why.

_____ 8. The 5 R's refer to nonverbal gesturing techniques.

_____ 9. Staff members should enhance or extend their leader's leadership style.

_____10. A good two-way communication network, with staff advisors, is important for successful leadership.

Turn to the back of the book to check your answers.

TOTAL CORRECT _____

5 Empower Followers— Apply the Mutual Reward Theory

Leadership is a process of mutual stimulation which, by the interplay of individual differences, controls human energy in the pursuit of a common goal.

P. Pigors

5 Empower Followers— Apply the Mutual Reward Theory

LEADERS PROVIDE SPECIAL REWARDS TO FOLLOWERS

A manager cannot become a leader without helping employees become followers. And a leader really cannot be a successful leader without *empowering followers*. But, first what is a follower? Is a follower really different from an employee? And how does a follower differ from an empowered follower?

The line that separates an employee from a follower is a fine one, and three factors are involved in the transition.

1. Employees cannot be forced or cajoled into becoming followers. It is purely voluntary on their part. If they want to move in the direction the leader has chosen, they join up. Naturally, they reason it is to their advantage to do so.

2. The vision projected by the leader is a primary persuader in helping employees become followers. The goal or mission must offer the promise of taking employees away from viewing work as work and raise expectations to such a level that following is considered natural and enjoyable.

3. The personality of the leader plays a significant role in the conversion of employees to followers. Sometimes charisma is present; sometimes it is not. However, there must be a degree of trust and a strong belief that life will become better as a follower than as an employee.

A fourth very simple, but extremely important, element is one that distinguishes followers from empowered followers and adds significantly to a leader's success. It is:

4. A leader who delegates both responsibility and authority to followers is empowering followers to take "ownership" of work and their actions. Accountability also must be an integral part of responsibility and authority. A leader also needs to learn how much authority should be "given away"—a balance that strengthens his or her leadership while promoting the highest level of empowerment for followers.

EMPOWERED FOLLOWERS EXTEND THE LEADER'S STYLE

All leaders go about helping employees become empowered followers in the leader's individual style.

When Mrs. Grayson took over the computerized office, no employee would have opted to follow the person she replaced. Six months later, when Mrs. Grayson was promoted within the company, almost every employee wanted to follow her to her new assignment. During the interim, Mrs. Grayson had created an exciting working environment, made each employee feel like a team member, raised levels of expectations, and shared both small and large victories in staff meetings and informal gatherings.

As one individual stated during a departure party: "It's hard to put your finger on it, but I felt better about myself under her leadership. My pay and benefits didn't change, but my attitude toward work and productivity certainly did. She provided rewards that are intangible."

HOW MANAGERS OFTEN VIEW EMPLOYEES

Managers are apt to view those under their supervision as owing them (or the company) productivity in return for pay and benefits. It is a contractual exchange system. The company attempts to provide a good working environment, fair treatment according to the laws, and as many psychological rewards as possible. In return, the employee produces according to accepted norms. Those who seek promotions (or are motivated by other reasons) produce more. Even under managers with good human relations skills, you hear such phrases as "another day at the office" and "another day, another dollar." Somehow, most employees feel "managed" and uninspired during their working hours.

HOW LEADERS VIEW EMPLOYEES

On the other hand, leaders train themselves to view employees as people who can become empowered followers, providing they are given a taste of victory. With this perspective, the leader is acknowledging that employees want to be led out of the typical work malaise. They want to be led, not managed—providing, of course, the demands on being a follower are within reason.

Employees do not want work to be work. It is not that they do not want to produce; they want a leader who will inspire them above and beyond the mundane tasks that constitute productivity. Employees who are given a role in decision making rise to an even higher level—empowerment. Those who reach this level are usually willing to produce at higher levels.

Just as employees respond differently to their manager, they also respond differently to their leader. If you complete the following exercise, you will be able to see how some employees view their managers and how some followers view their leaders. Keep in mind that a leader cannot expect all employees to be enthusiastic, empowered followers. Followers, nevertheless, seem to pull others along with them.

HOW EMPLOYEES VIEW MANAGERS VS. LEADERS

This exercise is designed to help you perceive how some employees view managers and how some followers view their leaders. If any of the views come close to fitting your environment (as an employee, manager, or leader), check the appropriate box.

Many employees view managers as superiors who are paid to control an operation, not lead it. Here are three typical employee attitudes.

☐ "I feel somewhat restricted and 'pegged' in my job. To satisfy my manager, all I need do is live up to my job description. It is all so mechanical. Despite all the co-workers that surround me, I often feel isolated. I need to sense I am going somewhere. I have lost my ability to lift myself up, and my manager does not seem to be concerned."

☐ "My manager often talks about a team effort, but little seems to happen to facilitate it. I work harder than others because I seek a promotion and a way out of my present condition. I am on friendly terms with my fellow workers, but I do not have a 'team' feeling. I think my manager is trying to do all the right things. She is as efficient, sensitive, and supportive as one could expect. It is just that there is so little to anticipate."

☐ "We have an outstanding manager, but frankly I still feel I am not accomplishing anything or really enjoying my job. It boils down to a matter of pride. I would like to feel I am part of a team that is winning a race that is important. I would like to break loose and contribute to something bigger so that everyone could share. I would like to brag to my family about what is happening to me on the job."

An employee who works under a leader and becomes a follower often has a different view.

☐ "When I worked under a manager, I felt like all of us were trying to hold a big rock up more than we were trying to push it an any direction. Now that I work for a leader, it is like we are all trying to push the rock over a cliff; and when it happens, we will all celebrate. I have never been a good team member, but I'm enjoying work more and producing at a higher level."

☐ "Since my transfer I find myself volunteering more. I am looking for ways to improve the operation even though I do not get credit. I believe the difference lies in having a leader instead of a manager. We have fun, but we also produce. I feel rewarded as a team member. It is not just a compliment now and then; it's a feeling of pride that we all share."

☐ "Frankly, if Mr. Harris were to be transferred, I would like to go with him. He generates so much excitement around here that other departments are envious. He seems to know what kinds of rewards make life better for us. It's not that other managers are not accessible, capable, and good to their people; it is just that Mr. Harris seems to be free of the management chains that keep others from being leaders. Yes, a few of our team would like to be back in their old comfortable ways. But not me!"

Exploring the strategies or techniques leaders use to convert employees into followers, especially empowered followers, is exciting. Although many factors are involved, the primary way to convert employees into followers is to practice the Mutual Reward Theory.

If you have ever observed two monkeys grooming each other, you have seen the Mutual Reward Theory (MRT) operating as its most basic level. When MRT works, both parties come out ahead. In the case of the monkeys, they both have something done for them that they cannot do effectively by themselves. Their lives are thereby enhanced.

MUTUAL REWARD THEORY

Your first reaction may be that MRT is no more than a truism, just another restatement of the old human relations principle: "If you scratch my back, I'll scratch yours."

When it comes to leadership, it is much more.

MRT states that a relationship between two people (or groups) is improved and enhanced when there is a satisfactory exchange of rewards between them. It is upon the human relations principle that all leader-follower relationships are built. Unless both parties (leader and follower) come out ahead, the relationship will not last. MRT is, therefore, one of the irreplaceable foundations of the Leadership Formula.

Receiving the right rewards makes followers want to follow. When followers follow with enthusiasm, leaders want to continue to lead. The following syllogism states the concept in a different way:

> People who want to lead must have followers.
> Followers support people who provide rewards.
> Therefore, people who want to become leaders
> must provide rewards.

Let's illustrate this dual-premise conclusion in a little different way. The first model below shows a typical reward exchange between a manager and a group of employees. It is less than ideal because the employees (at least in their opinion) are providing more rewards than the manager. Under this reward system, employees remain employees.

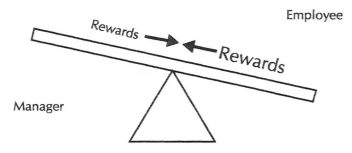

The second model below illustrates a better exchange mix. The manager is now a leader, and as a leader, has discovered and is providing more rewards. The balance bar is closer to the middle. Under the reward system, employees often convert themselves from employees into followers.

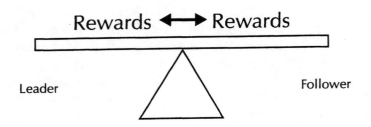

Rewards ←→ Rewards

Leader   Follower

It must be pointed out that leaders not only provide more rewards, they provide more appropriate rewards. For those employees who have become empowered followers, they usually are rewarded with greater decision-making power, more responsibility (still accompanied with accountability), and less supervision. Keep in mind that almost all rewards are psychological. Typical rewards are a sense of accomplishment and pride, a vision that often carries over into the follower's lifestyle, an *esprit de corps* in the workplace, self-esteem, and the feeling that comes from being a member of a group that has high standards and status.

GOOD LEADERS PROVIDE PRIMARY REWARDS

Leaders employ their listening skills to search out the "hot buttons," the rewards that empowered followers really want (not those that the leaders think they want or should have).

A single, highly prized reward is sometimes more valuable than a number of less important rewards. For example, in a city council election, voters might place a much greater value on better police protection than on any other issue. Police protection, therefore, becomes the primary reward; it overshadows less important, possible rewards (better schools, more senior citizen facilities). The candidates who promise better police protection, then, will receive the voters' support.

MISSING REWARDS

List three rewards your manager could easily provide but has not.

1. _____

2. _____

3. _____

Sometimes the primary rewards are the leaders themselves—or the principles or values they represent. Some people will follow leaders because they embody certain ideals or values, not because they offer pragmatic or practical rewards. Followership on ideals or values is true in all fields, but especially so in politics. Integrity, trust, and dependability should be viewed as significant rewards. When people continue to vote for an incumbent because she or he stands for the principles voters admire, the principles become the reward.

GOOD LEADERSHIP ITSELF IS A VALUED PRIMARY REWARD

Good leadership, then, is the best reward a leader can give to a follower. Nothing can take its place. Good leadership is often perceived by followers as a combination of certain qualities. You will discover many of these qualities by completing the exercise (Reward Checklist) that follows.

REWARD CHECKLIST

Different people look for different rewards from their leaders. Which rewards would you find most satisfying? Place a "1" by your first choice, and so on, until you have all 15 items ranked in importance. If you re-rank your choices with a friend or co-worker, you'll probably find the rewards that please you are similar to those that please others.

I would like a leader who

____ is honest and trustworthy.

____ is decisive and not wishy-washy.

____ has the ability to communicate in a clear, forceful manner.

____ provides special rewards that are important to me as an individual.

____ is flexible and who is willing to change when it is best for followers.

____ cannot be intimidated by others.

____ has statesmanlike qualities (someone who thinks of the long-term good and does not get involved in petty issues).

____ has compassion for others.

____ is consistent in actions and is reliable.

____ shows interest in my career prospects.

____ can relax and have fun at the right time.

____ gives me a compliment when I deserve it.

____ provides me with learning opportunities.

____ gives me a sense of pride in what I am doing.

____ has a personal talk with me now and then.

Add your own:

_____

_____

LEADERS CREATE SUPERIOR REWARD SYSTEMS

Making MRT work is not easy. It must be accepted as a major challenge. Leaders must provide motivating rewards. They must take into consideration that different followers may want different rewards; the more followers they have, the more complex the problem becomes.

To discover the right rewards, leaders must be outstanding listeners as well as be sensitive to both the needs of the organization and to the individuals in that organization. They must be able to send rewards to the right target areas at the right time. And then, because they cannot provide all the rewards followers desire, they must decide which rewards make the most sense in view of the situation. It is never a matter of providing all the rewards followers would like, but of providing the best rewards under the circumstances.

Dorothy Stansfield, the owner of a small electronics firm, called a meeting of her seventeen employees to discuss the rewards she was in a position to provide. She clearly stated that she could provide only one of the two rewards in each of the following categories:

* They could have higher salaries or more fringe benefits.
* She could spend more time with her employees in the plant, or she could spend more time developing orders in the field.
* They could have better working conditions now (costly improvements) or a new, far superior shop in the future.

Through open and prolonged discussion, with everyone having a voice, the decision was made to provide more benefits instead of a salary increase, more orders from the field instead of more personal attention, and a new shop in the future instead of improvements now. Once the meeting was over, Ms. Stansfield knew which rewards to provide. With good follow-through, she can now employ MRT to strengthen her organization and her leadership.

ALL LEADERS MUST DEVELOP THEIR OWN REWARD MATRIX

A leader of a sizable organization is going to have a strong, cohesive, winning organization if he or she can see that (1) the right personal rewards are provided to her or his immediate staff members; (2) all other personnel receive adequate personal rewards from their superiors; and (3) the right general rewards are provided to everyone in the organization. The result? The organization will produce more, and everyone will come out ahead.

To have a winning organization, leaders must develop their own reward matrix according to the goals of the organization and the needs of its members. The reward system, of course, is the crux of the matter. It is one thing to work out an individual mutual reward exchange where both people come out ahead; it is a far greater challenge to work out a group reward exchange where everybody comes out ahead. MRT does, however, offer this opportunity.

The governor of a state might give personal rewards to his or her immediate staff and to the members of both houses of the legislature. The governor must also give general rewards to the voters in the state. The president of a college might concentrate on personal rewards for immediate staff, faculty members, and key administrators. General rewards would be provided to students, alumni, and members of the community.

President Eisenhower gave voters some of the key rewards they wanted in the early and mid-fifties. His reputation as a military leader, his Midwestern brand of conservatism, and his undeniable patriotism appealed to an electorate worried about the Korean War and the threat of international communism.

Some political observers believe that President Carter, as another example, may have miscalculated the rewards voters wanted when he placed so much emphasis on world peace at the expense of domestic matters. Many people, perhaps more than he and his staff recognized, wanted the reward of a stronger economy and safer cities.

Most followers realize that they are not going to get all the rewards they want, but they want those with high priority to receive first attention. The choice of which rewards to provide (and the relative success at providing them) has a lot to do with the final ratings presidents receive in history books.

Followers always determine the destiny of their leaders. And the key to a good reward system is: *the right mix of the right rewards at the right time.*

Personal rewards are rewards a leader gives to either a single follower or a small group of followers. Examples are one-on-one conversations, special attention, and individualized forms of recognition. All leaders can and should provide personal rewards to their immediate staff.

PERSONAL VS. GENERAL REWARDS

What about leaders who have hundreds, thousands, or millions of followers?

Here the leader must also provide general rewards. A general reward is almost always bestowed impersonally (e.g., in a company memo or an announcement from the dean's office). Needless to say, a general reward must be designed to please the majority of followers. Some obvious examples of general rewards are tax cuts (government), holidays (school administration), end-of-year bonuses (business), and cost-of-living increases (labor).

It is therefore important that top leaders make sure that their subordinates offer personal rewards to those they lead so that everyone in the group receives both personal and general rewards. General rewards, as welcome as they may be, will not replace the need for personal rewards from the immediate leader.

YOUR LEADERSHIP IS SHOWING

The Presence of Leadership

Rick, the leader of a highly successful rock group for five years, provided the following several rewards to his other four group members: good musical arrangements, good bookings, and ample opportunities for individual recognition. In return, his musicians were dependable, made maximum use of their talent, and supported him as their leader in all crucial tests. Rick demonstrated his leadership by insisting that the reward system that was implemented be discussed openly so that everyone understood the tradeoff involved.

Marty discovered quickly that if her fashion boutique were to survive, she would not be able to pay more than minimum wages to her part-time staff. How could she compensate? She discussed with employees how she could provide some rewards and not others. Together they decided the best reward would be to prepare them for higher-paying, more demanding fashion jobs elsewhere. Marty implemented the reward suggestion by taking each employee on a buying trip, having a monthly luncheon with lots of fashion conversation, and giving each more opportunities to learn about the business. She demonstrated her leadership ability and implemented a reward system that doubled her employees' performance.

The Absence of Leadership

Joyce was a human resource director for a large branch of a successful retail chain. She reported directly to a corporate vice president. Over a period of three years, Joyce did more than her part in going the extra mile for her superior's benefit. She researched and introduced some cost-effective procedures; she cut down on personnel turnover; and, most important of all, she solved all these problems without going to the corporate office for help. But Joyce received little recognition from the corporate officer—the one reward she wanted most. As a result, Joyce finally moved to a competitor's company.

Drew was more than upset when he lost his job as restaurant manager. After all, he had a college degree in restaurant management and had devoted seven years of his life to working his way up to manager. So why did the vice president fire Drew? It was because of low employee morale and low productivity as well as excessive customer complaints. Investigation into the matter showed that Drew had neither discussed (nor provided) a reward system for his employees. His attitude was that if employees did well, he would reward them with a promotion. He demonstrated his lack of leadership by not discovering and providing daily as well as long-term rewards.

The larger the organization, the more critical is the need for a good delivery network to make certain that rewards reach their destination. In this respect, MRT is dependent upon the quality of the communication system within the organization. But MRT, if practiced with vigor and sensitivity, can also make a contribution in improving the communication skills of both leaders and followers. Here are some reasons why:

COMMUNICATION AND GENERAL REWARDS

* Making MRT work forces a leader to become a better listener. You simply cannot provide the right rewards until you know what people want. You find these rewards only when you search and listen.
* Setting up a reward system with an individual forces both parties to get together to exchange views, negotiate, and learn more about each other.
* People who must depend upon the media to receive rewards from their leaders listen more and respond better when the leader talks about rewards that are important to them—rewards that are uncovered as a result of research and listening.

The number one side benefit of MRT is better communication. Leaders should practice MRT for no better reason than for improving communication alone.

Leaders help develop nonfollowers into followers through the way they employ MRT in specific situations. They fail as leaders when they ignore or do not capitalize on the power of MRT. The cases at the end of this chapter illustrate what happens when leaders incorporate—or fail to incorporate—MRT into their style.

If MRT is to work, leaders must also receive rewards. In one sense, leaders should not expect as many rewards as followers because certain rewards are automatically built into leadership positions. For example, a psychic payoff takes place the moment one becomes a leader. Some of it comes from the follower recognition, but most of it stems from the exercise of power. Most top-level leaders function in a rather intoxicating environment. That is, although highly rewarding, power can be dangerous. Consider the following comment from the owner of a manufacturing concern.

WHAT REWARDS DO LEADERS RECEIVE?

> The heady wine of leadership can send anyone on a disaster trip. The higher the position, the stronger the wine. Beginning leaders must learn to sit on their egos by reminding themselves that leaders are just normal human beings who are supposed to serve their followers and not their own egos. It is not an easy lesson to learn, and as leaders move into more rarefied atmospheres, they must learn it over and over again. The problem is one

of balance. Leaders must have strong egos to lead; they must also keep thinking well of themselves so they can maintain their personal confidence and continue to lead. But they must eventually learn to live comfortably with the power that is theirs, or their followers will either hope for a fall or actually create it.

Because of the built-in rewards of leadership, leaders should recognize that they will probably give more rewards than they will receive. Leaders should keep in mind that it is sometimes awkward for their subordinates to reward them with more than loyalty and performance. For example, members of the group may want to give their leaders compliments. But because of peer pressure and lack of opportunity, they do not get around to doing so. Leaders who think that their followers are not appreciative should remember two things: If followers had the opportunity, they would probably provide more personal rewards to their leader. If they didn't appreciate the leader, they probably would not be following.

None of this is to say that the leader-follower relationship should not be mutually rewarding. It should. It simply states that there is not perfect parity in the mutual reward system.

MRT MOTIVATES BOTH PARTIES

Many definitions of leadership state that a true leader is one who can motivate others. L. L. Bernard gave us this definition in 1926: "Any person who is more than ordinarily efficient in carrying psychological stimuli to others and is thus effective in conditioning collective responses may be called a leader."

Bernard's definition is a simple restatement of the basic premise of the Mutual Reward Theory. When followers receive the appropriate stimuli (rewards), they in turn reward the leader with a positive response. The process can continue indefinitely. The positive responses of the followers elicit more positive stimuli, which in turn create more positive responses. Everyone comes out ahead.

THE ULTIMATE FRANCHISE TO LEAD COMES FROM FOLLOWERS

Followers make leaders when they agree to follow. Followers break leaders when they change their minds. Followers, and followers alone, provide the franchise to lead. Organizations may appoint leaders, but the ultimate source of power comes from followers. Leadership is therefore the ability to attract and keep followers. Keeping followers is why it is important to empower them to expand the leader's effectiveness. Unfortunately, all it takes is a few hostile nonfollowers to determine the power of a leader. That is why leaders must constantly maintain healthy surveillance. When trouble starts, they need to move in quickly and discover the rewards that will get everyone on the right track again.

Ultimately, the Mutual Reward Theory will not work if it is used to strengthen the leader's position at the expense of the followers. Followers soon discover when a leader is self-serving. If rewards, both personal and general, do not have a true ring, they will not be accepted. If MRT is used simply to manipulate followers, it will surely fail.

As one leader commented, "You might be able to manage without a heart, but you cannot lead effectively without one."

SUMMARY

* Successful leaders develop employees and followers into empowered followers—people who are given authority along with responsibility and accountability.
* The Mutual Reward Theory is the human relations foundation for the Leadership Formula and gives any leadership style more substance.
* Leaders must constantly monitor and improve their reward matrix on behalf of followers.
* It is not only providing the right number of rewards that makes a good leader, it is providing the *right* rewards.
* Both personal and general rewards must be provided to followers; the further away the leader is from his or her followers, the more important general rewards become.
* The best reward a leader can provide a follower is good leadership; the best reward a follower can provide a leader is productivity.
* The more valuable the rewards, the fewer are required.
* A good way for a leader to restore a relationship with a follower is to discover a *better* reward system.
* The better the reward system works, the more motivated each party becomes.
* MRT should not be used to manipulate followers in an unfair way.

Case 9: Compassion

Ralph and Randy were discussing the Mutual Reward Theory on the way home from a professional conference. The theory was introduced by one of the conference speakers. Ralph is Randy's team leader.

"Randy," said Ralph, "I'm of the opinion that most good leaders automatically practice the Mutual Reward Theory."

"I'm not so sure," replied Randy. "In our company, I feel we provide too few rewards for our employees and not always the right ones. We have too much employee turnover needlessly."

"Are you saying that if I and the other leaders in our organization would apply the theory that we would be more productive?"

"Yes, I believe that would be true."

"It is too contrived," stated Ralph. "I believe all we need do is demonstrate compassion and concern. When employees know how we feel about them, the rewards are obvious. We don't have to list the rewards."

Randy replied: "I agree that the theory won't work without compassion, but I don't believe compassion will do it alone. We can't build a good reward system without knowing what our employees want. We need a more realistic approach if everybody is to come out ahead. For example, I believe it would greatly improve our personal relationship if we could sit down and talk about the rewards we both seek. You are the leader and I am the follower. What rewards should I provide? What should I expect from you in return?"

"Perhaps you are right. It might make me a better leader. I'm not so sure, however, that it will be easy for me to do."

Would you recommend that Ralph make a major attempt to weave MRT into his approach as a team leader? Because he believes in compassion and concern for people, would it be easier for him than someone else? Would he be more successful than someone else? What are the chances, in your opinion, that he will make the behavioral changes necessary? (The authors' opinions are in the back of the book.)

Tom Castelletti is the manager of a trucking depot for a large firm. He supervises about sixty truckers and sixteen maintenance people. A high school dropout, he has earned his role as a manager the hard way, starting out as a trucker himself. Bill Nelson, the owner and a strong supporter of Tom, wants him to blend the Mutual Reward Theory into his rough, but effective management style. He feels it will improve productivity and create a better relationship with the union. Tom is reluctant to make the move for the following reasons.

Case 10: Fear

Tom says; "The moment I start talking about rewards around here, they'll want the sky. The first thing will be more money, then better hours. It will open up a whole can of worms. The idea may be okay in some places, but not around here. We deal in a more basic way with people. They need more discipline, not less. They would just laugh at this approach."

Bill replies: "Tom, I don't think you get the point. There's nothing to be afraid of. Everyone needs certain rewards from their jobs. Some of these rewards you can provide with little effort if you take the trouble to find out what they are. Others may be beyond your power to provide, and you should just say so. All you are doing now is putting out fires. By working out reward systems with your key people and finding out what the truckers really want, you'll be able to do a much better job with less effort. You'll discover when you open up the subject on a person-to-person basis that the individual will ask for fewer rewards than you suspect. What it boils down to is a kind of relationship contract. If you'll produce for me, I'll do my best to provide the rewards you want. It's a very practical approach."

Bill continues: "I'll tell you what I am willing to do. Let's you and I sit down and work out a better reward system between ourselves. You tell me what rewards you want, and I'll do the same. If it works for us, will you be willing to try it on your truckers?"

Will Bill's approach work? Or are Tom's fears justified? Can MRT work in all environments? (See the back of the book for the authors' opinions.)

Self-Test   Mark each statement True (T) or False (F).

_____ 1. Leaders empower followers by giving them authority in addition to responsibility and accountability.

_____ 2. You always know when MRT is working because both parties come out ahead.

_____ 3. A single high-level reward can sometimes equal or replace many smaller rewards.

_____ 4. Generally speaking, leaders provide all the rewards followers need.

_____ 5. Anyone who can make MRT work on a day-to-day basis will substantially improve his or her communication skills.

_____ 6. The ultimate franchise to lead comes from the organization.

_____ 7. MRT is the human relations foundation of the Leadership Formula; if one ignores it, the other foundations are rendered less effective.

_____ 8. Providing the right rewards is often more important than providing a great number of rewards.

_____ 9. MRT is easy to apply.

_____10. The best general reward a leader can provide is to be a good leader.

Turn to the back of the book to check your answers.

TOTAL CORRECT _____

6 Expand Your Power of Influence

The great principle of all is that no one of either sex should be without a commander.

Plato, Laws XII

⋆ 6 Expand Your Power of Influence

LEADERS KNOW WHEN AND HOW TO GET TOUGH

You will recall from earlier discussion that the Mutual Reward Theory is an expression of the human relations side of leadership. Human relations is the softer side of MRT. Structure and discipline are parameters of the other side of leadership—the harder side. The two sides work together. MRT increases the group's tolerance for organizational structure; structure provides the discipline necessary to get the job done. Both are equally important. In fact, one is totally ineffective without the other.

The key to leadership is finding the blend of the two sides of MRT—that balance that will work. It is a tightrope every leader and manager must walk daily, as the following example illustrates.

> The success of Ruth Reynolds' business college is a known fact in the community. Mrs. Reynolds started her school in a dilapidated downtown location seven years ago. Two months ago, the college moved into new, modern facilities to handle a student body which has increased 30 percent a year for three successive years. Why has Mrs. Reynolds been so successful? Perhaps because of her well-balanced blend of personal concern for staff and students and her discipline.
>
> Mrs. Reynolds devotes a considerable amount of time to MRT counseling—with both staff and students. One of her most common questions is, "What can I do for you that I am not doing already?" But there is never any doubt about who is in charge. She sets a work tempo that others emulate. And if someone does not live up to standards, she intervenes quickly and talks openly about it.
>
> One instructor made this statement: "She has that rare combination of personal touch and powerful leadership. I never feel neglected or unrewarded, but I also know I must live up to my potential. She can be tough when it's required."

Authority, structure, and discipline contribute to the framework of any successful group or organization. They are the tools of control. They prevent disorganization and chaos.

Without such a framework, there will be squabbles, dissension, and confusion. Any group, no matter what its members might say, needs structure. If provided in the right amount and in the right way, most people welcome and respect it.

If you, like many people, feel the words authority and discipline have a negative connotation, it is because people connect authority and discipline with a loss of freedom. However, authority and discipline should be positive words to would-be leaders. They are the vehicles that will permit leaders to express their leadership.

Everyone must, at times, let his or her power show. Authority must be communicated. Structure must be imposed. Timing is important, as the following two cases illustrate.

Everyone was amazed when Jeff received the football head-coach appointment. He was sensitive to the needs of others and a gifted strategist, but people thought he was too soft to be a head coach. Jeff said little for the first two days, letting people react and adjust. Then he called a meeting of the entire team—players and assistant coaches. He sat on a table and stared at his audience for ten minutes until everyone settled down and decided to listen. Jeff then said: "Everyone in this room has a choice. You must decide whether to accept my authority or drop off the team today. Things will be different around here effective immediately. We are going to do whatever it takes to put a winning team together. If you are out on the field in ten minutes, I'll know you are with me." He then turned and walked away.

Jeff had, through very few words, expressed his leadership. He drew a line. From that moment on everyone, including the other coaches, knew who was in charge. Jeff was still the nice guy he had always been, but he was now a leader as well.

EXPRESSING LEADERSHIP

Lorna Henderson accepted her new position as superintendent of the nursing home knowing that she was walking into a hornet's nest. She spent her first two days being friendly, but efficient. On the third day, she scheduled ten-minute private talks with each member of her staff.

There was a constant stream of people in and out of her office for six hours. In each interview she made a statement similar to this: "You will find me fair, and I will give you all the rewards and personal time possible. I care about your future, but I have standards that you must live up to. If you do not accept them, I will take corrective action. I intend to turn this nursing home around in sixty days. Once this happens, it will be a much better place for you to work. Are there any questions?"

Leaders must maintain control. If they do not, the members of the group begin to go in different directions, and the group becomes fragmented instead of cohesive. If disorder continues, anarchy sets in. The purpose of leadership is to get people to work together toward common goals—to accomplish things that can only be achieved through group effort. The effective leader can make a group achieve more than the sum of its members' individual efforts. None of this can happen, however, without structure. All leaders must at one time or another tighten the reins, stand firm, and take corrective action.

Leadership is, says Ralph Stogdill, "the initiation and maintenance of structure in expectation and interaction." This definition implies that the leader is responsible for the development of the structure necessary to maximize group performance in the achievement of organizational goals.

MANAGERS AND LEADERS MUST MAINTAIN STRUCTURE

But creating structure and maintaining it do not mean to return to old-fashioned, autocratic forms of leadership. Structure does not mean harsh, arbitrary rules that subordinates must adhere to or else, nor paternalistic leadership, where all group members are expected to honor their leaders whether they deserve it or not. If a Theory X* leadership style doesn't produce the results a leader anticipated, it does not mean that she or he should embrace Theory Y.* Clear, decisive leadership and MRT will keep the group headed in the right direction, regardless of leadership style.

There is no escape from the fact that every leader must walk that tight line between freedom and control. The Boy Scout leader must give the members of the troop the freedom to exercise initiative, but exert enough control so that they do not get out of hand. The teacher cannot help students reach learning goals without discipline and respect. The corporate president must run a tight ship in order to reach established productivity and profit goals. Even the President of the United States must occasionally take time to do some corrective counseling with an errant cabinet or staff member. Authority must be expressed. No leader can avoid understanding structure. It goes with the territory.

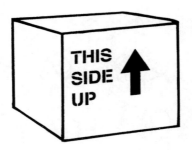

LEADERS DRAW AN AUTHORITY LINE

All leaders establish an authority line, an imaginary, psychological demarcation between acceptable and unacceptable behavior. It says to organization members, "I will go along with this, but I will draw the line when it comes to that." It is a form of communication (perhaps never verbalized) that says, in effect: "You have all the freedom you need to perform effectively and enjoy yourself, but there is a limit. If you go beyond my authority line, you can expect some form of discipline." An authority line can also be interpreted as a dual-edged sword, that is, "I respect you and your individual rights and will support you enthusiastically, providing you stay within reasonable bounds."

From a group member's point of view, an authority line can be tested: "I will try to get by with as much as possible, even if I step over the line. It won't hurt my progress in the long run." From a leader's point of view, an authority line states: "We have a contract here. I want to provide as much freedom as possible, but I must also maintain control. I am the leader and I must lead. If matters reach a certain point, I will step in. I am willing to provide certain rewards, but my return from you is a certain standard of behavior."

When a subordinate honors a leader's authority line, the subordinate is giving that leader a reward: accepting his or her leadership. When

---

Theory X, management by control, states that workers must be directed and controlled in order to achieve high productivity. Theory Y, participatory management, states that workers will achieve greater productivity if they can direct their own efforts through involvement with organizational goals.

a leader has good followership, the successful leader provides more rewards to followers—more freedom and authority, greater decision making, and similar types of rewards. The reward exchange is mutually beneficial (MRT in practice); and everyone benefits from knowing where the authority line is. Followers become empowered followers which, in turn, enhances the leader's style.

How and where an authority line is set is a crucial part of anyone's leadership style. It demonstrates how much leadership is present and how sensitive the leader is in employing it.

Is it possible for a leader to draw a line that will be accepted by all group members, provide the structure needed, and help the group reach predetermined goals? If so, must the line be raised or lowered as conditions change?

To answer these questions, let's look at two widely different examples of authority-line violations.

As a manager, for instance, it may not bother you if an employee is occasionally late in returning from lunch—say, a few minutes once or twice a week. Your personal tolerance level—related to the authority line you establish—can handle this. But if the same person is 15 or 20 minutes late two or three times a week, you may feel that your tolerance *threshold* has been crossed, that your authority line has been violated, and some form of discipline is in order. You may say to yourself: "This person does not recognize my leadership role or honor my authority line. My authority is being questioned, and it is time to act. This person is no longer behaving in a manner I can accept."

As a result, you initiate a corrective interview. By taking some corrective action, you have accomplished three things. First, you have used your authority (power) to remind everyone that you have standards. Second, you have adjusted your authority line as far as recent violations are concerned. Third, and most important, you have clearly expressed your leadership.

Although the individual disciplined might react in a negative manner, your other employees might say: "I like the way he leads the department. He doesn't let a few people get away with murder. I just don't like a boss whom people can intimidate." Although readjusting a line may upset violators, it provides necessary group structure. The overall response, at least in the long run, is usually positive.

The President of the United States, in the role as head of the government, has established a kind of authority line with several other countries. He might state, for example, that if a certain geographical frontier is crossed, a specific action will be taken in response. The United States has a national tolerance level, and once it has been breached (for example, the invasion of an ally), some form of action can be anticipated.

KNOWING WHEN AND WHERE TO DRAW THE LINE

The setting and maintenance of authority lines—whether between two leaders or between a leader and a group—is a characteristic of leadership.

A manager or leader must follow through and take the promised action when her or his authority is violated. If follow through is lacking or lightly considered, the manager or leader loses credibility. A discipline or authority line should not be set in the first place unless it can be upheld. Inactivity or indecision is always interpreted as an absence of leadership.

> **LEADERSHIP**   A SUCCESSFUL LEADER KNOWS AND PRACTICES THE DEFINITION OF LEADERSHIP.
> A COMMON DEFINITION OF *LEADERSHIP* IS *THE SENSITIVE USE OF POWER TO ACHIEVE GROUP GOALS.*

All leaders have power—some more abundantly than others—but it is the way power is exercised that determines whether or not the leader is successful.

MAINTAINING AN AUTHORITY LINE

There are sensitive and insensitive ways to establish and maintain a clear, firm authority line. A sensitive way protects the self-esteem of the follower so that he or she accepts the message of the leader and remains a follower. An insensitive way can turn an enthusiastic follower into a disenchanted employee. Listed below are twelve techniques or approaches frequently used to maintain authority lines. Check those that you feel will do more harm than good and then match your choices with a classmate or friend.

___Ask politely for follower cooperation.

___Reprimand violators openly so that everyone gets the message quickly.

___Stand tough on previous decisions so everyone knows you mean business.

___Communicate strong leadership through image projection; circulate in a friendly manner, but let your presence indicate that you are in command.

___Speak with authority.

___Discipline individual violators in private counseling sessions.

___Conduct periodic group meetings in which you encourage discussion, but show you are in charge.

___Be extra tough on immediate staff, and then delegate maintenance of your authority line to them so that you can appear more benevolent to followers.

___Stay with the philosophy that the fewer rules the better, as long as group goals are met. Fewer rules mean less maintenance.

___Use the group reprimand approach—if the shoe fits, let the follower wear it.

___Take care of violations immediately—before you magnify them out of proportion and before the behavior in question becomes a habit with the violator.

___Communicate your displeasure without words—let your negative countenance or body language convey the message.

Power CAN provide opportunitiesfor leadership, but it doesn't come with a set of instructions for using it wisely. No warranty is provided. Some leaders fail to use the power they possess while others abuse it; only a few learn to use it skillfully. Establishing an authority line and then protecting it is not the only way a leader expresses power. Power manifests itself in communication, delegation of assignments, and especially in decision making. But nothing impresses subordinates more quickly and clearly than a leader who protects his or her authority line with conviction.

EXERCISING POWER

    A fundamental difference between mangers and leaders is the way they develop and utilize their power. Both may maintain structure and discipline lines, and understand the authority-line concept, but they exercise their power in different ways. To understand how and why this happens, it is necessary to evaluate power sources.

The three basic sources of leadership power are (1) role power (the power that goes with the position), (2) personality power (power generated by the force of the individual), and (3) knowledge power (power that is derived from special skills or knowledge).

THREE SOURCES OF LEADERSHIP POWER

    In exercising leadership, all sources of power are always present. You cannot rely totally on any single source. But, to gain better follower reaction, it is sometimes best to soft-pedal one source and emphasize another.

    Consider some of these examples of power sources: A military officer may derive 70 percent of her or his power from the position itself (role power), 20 percent from personality power, 10 percent from expert power. In a combat assignment, the officer's leadership power derives primarily from rank (role). In a noncombat assignment, it probably is expertise or personality that substantially affects, positively or negatively, the leader's image.

    In contrast, a clergy or leader of a church may derive 50 percent of his or her power from personality, 30 percent from knowledge, and 20 percent from the role itself.

POWER ANALYSIS

All leaders make use of all three power sources; however, some positions call for more emphasis on one source than another. (Also, there is the shifting of power sources according to the situation.) What, in your opinion, would be a reasonable percentage breakdown of the power sources in these leadership roles?

	Lab Manager	Movie Director	Girl Scout Leader
Role Power	____%	____%	____%
Personality Power	____%	____%	____%
Knowledge Power	____%	____%	____%
	====	====	====
	100%	100%	100%

Compare the percentages you assigned to each of the three leadership roles with the responses of your classmates. Discuss the reasons why (or why not) your responses differ or are similar to others. Then, draw some conclusions from the discussion.

THE EFFECTIVE USE OF ROLE POWER

The power attached to a leadership position, in most situations, is more potent than the person who occupies it realizes. For example, the position of President of the United States has awesome power—no matter who occupies it. The same is true of corporate and college presidents, police chiefs, and other government officials. Even the first-line supervisor or volunteer leader has more role power than she or he suspects.

Role power is generally accepted without question. People know it is not easy to be in a position of authority; in fact, they are often sympathetic to those who are. (How often have you heard someone say about the President, "I wouldn't have his job if they paid me ten million dollars a year!") People, however, do not react well to leaders who abuse their power. They resent the coach, the senator, or the boss who takes advantage of the power engendered by her or his role or position. The coach who bullies players, the senator who doesn't vote on key issues, or the boss who betrays employee trust will soon find himself or herself without followers.

Thus, an astute leader will not rely on role power alone. Successful leadership is effective only when a leader practices other good leadership principles (maximizing the Leadership Formula). That is why, generally speaking, the best way to use role power is to let it work silently.

Live with that power comfortably and use it gracefully. Recognize it, but don't let it go to your head.

Keep in mind that role or position power is there to be used and should be communicated without hesitation under certain circumstances. For example, when an authority line needs to be clearly indicated or lowered, no other source of power will reestablish the leader's authority more quickly. Consider the following examples of role power.

> Frankly, the difference between you and me is that I am sitting in the chair of the president. You don't have to like me as a person, but you must respect my position. From now on I expect you to conform to policy like everyone else.

> Okay, everybody. We made excellent progress last month, but we still need to eliminate some safety violations. Keep in mind that my position forces me to take disciplinary action if necessary. The same would be true if you had my job.

> There is nothing personal about it, but as long as I occupy this position, that's the way it will be. No exceptions.

ROLE POWER	GENERALLY SPEAKING, LEADERS ARE GENTLE IN THE USE OF ROLE POWER. THEY DOWNPLAY THE SOURCE. WHEN THEY DO USE IT, THEY DRAW A FIRM LINE AND QUICKLY MOVE ON TO THE UTILIZATION OF OTHER SOURCES.

CAPITALIZING ON PERSONALITY POWER

Every individual—whether in a leadership role or not—has personality power. We can all use our personalities to influence others. Those who have a positive attitude, a pleasant voice, a decisive manner, and confidence frequently have the most impact.

Charisma is the term frequently used to describe those people whose personalities are like magnets and draw others to them. Charisma, according to *Webster's New World Dictionary*, is a "special quality of leadership that captures the popular imagination and inspires unswerving allegiance and devotion." Some leaders have charisma in abundance; others have none. Movie stars who have it are winners at the box office; politicians who do not have it may find it difficult to get elected.

Charismatic people have a star quality that makes people want to follow them—two good examples are Princess Diana (of Wales) and Martin Luther King. Charisma is great for those who possess it. If you do not have charisma, however, it does not mean that you have *no* personality power. You do.

Personality power becomes important in positions of leadership that are inherently weak in role power. For example, many teachers recognize that their role as classroom leader does not have high power content, so they tap their personality power more heavily. They do not say, "Look, I'm the teacher so what I say goes." Rather, they skillfully employ their personality power to achieve high learning levels.

Capitalizing on personality power is also true of many who are in leadership roles—volunteer leaders, ministers, and elected leaders in trade, fraternal, and social organizations. They get more voltage from the power of their personalities than from the roles they occupy.

LEADERSHIP AND CHARISMA

Rate the following Presidents (on a scale of one through ten) on their leadership ability and charisma.

Leadership		*Charisma*
_____	Harry Truman	_____
_____	Dwight Eisenhower	_____
_____	John Kennedy	_____
_____	Lyndon Johnson	_____
_____	Richard Nixon	_____
_____	Gerald Ford	_____
_____	Jimmy Carter	_____
_____	Ronald Reagan	_____
_____	George Bush	_____
_____	Bill Clinton	_____

Study your ratings. Is there any correlation—either positive or negative—between leadership and charisma? What conclusions can you draw about the role charisma plays in the development of leadership qualities?

The contrast between role or position power and personality power, no doubt, cannot be characterized better than in comparing the presidential candidates in the 1980 National Democratic Convention. President Carter leaned heavily on his role as President and head of the Democratic Party, whereas Senator Kennedy leaned heavily on his personality power. The leadership profiles communicated were different because the power sources were different.

When a "power personality" occupies a "power role," you always have the possibility of outstanding leadership, provided that both power sources are used effectively. And, of course, a positive attitude is paramount to maximizing personality power.

PERSONALITY POWER	IN MOST CASES, LEADERS USE THEIR PERSONALITY POWER TO INSPIRE AND PERSUADE FOLLOWERS. MANAGERS, ON THE OTHER HAND, FALL BACK ON THEIR ROLE POWER TO ACHIEVE PRODUCTIVITY.

When a leader has special skills and knowledge to back up the leadership role he or she occupies, an additional source of power is generated. Expertise is knowledge power. People like to be led by those who know the answers. They look up to those with expertise, giving them more authority than they would otherwise possess.

MAKING THE MOST OF KNOWLEDGE POWER

Knowledge—real or imagined—is power. Being recognized as an expert gives you additional clout. True expertise, then, generates power automatically.

In some situations, knowledge power can be more important than any other kind. For example, the pilot of an airliner is the captain (role power); he or she may have a strong personal presence (personality power); but it is the ability to fly the plane safely that is the source of the pilot's primary power. When the sky is rough, skill is what counts—not the title or charm the pilot may possess.

Leadership itself is expertise. Many times leadership skills are valued more highly than technical competence. In fact, in most high-level leadership roles, one is more likely to find people with leadership skills than technical competence. The best engineer in the world cannot run an engineering firm without leadership ability. The winning combination, of course, is leadership capabilities *and* technical knowledge.

The primary danger for those who possess expertise is relying on it too heavily. The know-it-all leader soon loses both friends and followers. The leader who refuses to listen is quickly in trouble. But the leader who has both technical expertise and leadership ability has a definite edge. Sometimes knowledge can be the primary source of power, as this case illustrates:

Brenda majored in mathematics and minored in computer science in college. It turned out to be a perfect combination because she was hired by a computer manufacturer the day after graduation. In less than two years, Brenda was offered a job with a competitor—a client organization. The board of the client company wanted someone to manage those who were going to operate the computer equipment they had bought from Brenda's firm. She took the job, at a big jump in pay and a drop in status. She was given the title of acting manager, which diminished her role power. On top of this, Brenda was a rather quiet, unassuming, work-oriented person. She would be the first to admit that she had little personality power. So Brenda relied heavily—almost 90 percent—on her knowledge of what she was doing.

It didn't take long for those in her department to sense how lucky they were to have Brenda as an acting manager. She seemed to be able to come up with the solution to any computer or programming problem. In addition, she was a great teacher. She always took time to explain how things operate and why it was wiser to do something one way than another. Because of her knowledge (and her ability to communicate it), Brenda earned the respect of her subordinates without having a great deal of role or personality power.

Soon thereafter Brenda was appointed manager of the computer center (no longer acting). She found herself becoming more confident because of the positive feedback she received from the people in her department. But even after she gained more role and personality power, she was still respected (and followed) primarily because of her knowledge. She had, for that department at least, the right blend of power for a leadership style.

Technical and scientific experts, as well as other specialists, are often short on personality power. Many a research and development person has been promoted into a leadership role, only to request a transfer back to the laboratory or design team. Many an outstanding salesperson has tried the role of sales manager, only to return to the field. In such cases, it is usually a failure to understand or use the elements that make a power base.

KNOWLEDGE POWER

ALTHOUGH LEADERS AND MANAGERS MAY HAVE THE SAME LEVEL OF KNOWLEDGE POWER, LEADERS OFTEN SPEND MORE TIME TEACHING FOLLOWERS WHAT THEY KNOW. LEADERS AS TEACHERS GAIN RESPECT, LOYALTY, AND PRODUCTIVITY. MANAGERS SEEM TO TAKE THEIR KNOWLEDGE FOR GRANTED; THUS, THEY SHARE IT LESS.

POWER OF INFLUENCE PROFILES

Two profiles, one of a manager and the other of a leader, are illustrated below. A typical profile of a manager with a strong power of influence package might be similar to the illustration on the left. You will observe that many managers, perhaps most, rely heavily on their role power. A few consider it their only power source. In contrast, many apparently fail to develop their personality power. Some, perhaps because they lack self-confidence, permit their personality power to dry up under the details, procedures, and red tape associated with the management marshmallow. Even knowledge power is ignored by some managers when, in fact, they have more power than leaders in comparable roles. A few managers render themselves less effective because they do not "keep up" with developments. When effectiveness is low, respect often disintegrates.

In contrast, a typical power of influence profile for a successful leader is more apt to approximate the illustration on the right. Many leaders try not to use their role power, believing it may have a more negative impact on followers than personality power. Leaders who prefer to downplay their role or position power, claim that people are more willing to accept personality power than the raw power that comes from occupying a position. Leaders with charisma obviously make the most of their personalities.

POWER OF INFLUENCE

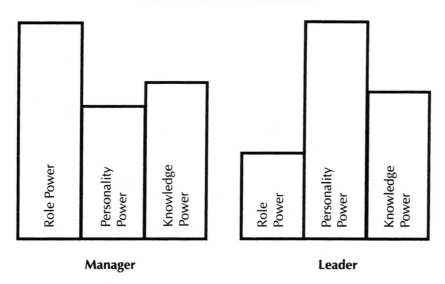

Some leaders, but not all, make better use of knowledge power than do managers. Not only do they try to keep ahead of followers in technical data, but they do a superior job of teaching what they know and communicating in general.

Although managers and leaders alike can benefit from a periodic review of how they are utilizing their power of influence, those who feel boxed in as managers might free themselves by revamping their profiles along the lines of the typical leader. In changing their profiles, however, they should be careful to strike a "balance" of the power sources within their comfort zone.

BALANCING YOUR POWER PROFILE

The best way to use the power inherent in your role is to occupy your position with ease, grace, and confidence. Power goes with the role, but your projection of "presence" either increases or decreases your authority.

You increase your personality power by learning how to capitalize on your strong traits and strengthening your weak ones.

You increase your knowledge power by learning more about the technology and skills in your special area. The more you know, the more you will be able to communicate to subordinates. The more knowledge you communicate, the more respect (and power) they will give you.

In any situation, the leader should draw upon all power sources available to him or her. The power sources cannot be clearly separated. The leader, however, can often be more effective if he or she uses one source of power to dominate his or her leadership style.

To provide practice in how different power sources might be emphasized in different situations, complete the following exercise. Read the situation first; then select the one or two sources of power you feel would best accomplish the task at hand with as little negative reaction as possible.

INCREASING YOUR POWER BASE

Managers and leaders can increase their power base regardless of their situation. The first possibility, of course, is promotion into a more powerful role. Increasing your personality power is a more personal matter. Although courses in communication, public speaking, and self-analysis are helpful, personality enhancement must in the end be a do-it-yourself project. And increasing your knowledge power can be accomplished on campus, as you earn a higher degree; on the job, through seminars and work projects; and individually, through self-study.

Successful managers usually strive to increase their power base; leaders often make a greater effort in expanding their power of influence. Leaders know that the stronger their power base, the more leadership they can put into their style.

It is an understatement to say that followers study their leaders carefully and are more sensitive to how leaders use power than most leaders realize. Although group members may not respond immediately to their leader's use, or abuse, of power (they may be busy adjusting to a new authority line or working harder to reach a group goal), the image they form of the leader is, in large part, determined by the way that leader handles power.

Handling power is an important factor when you consider that the ultimate source of a leader's power is the people he or she leads.

POWER SOURCE EXERCISE

Listed below are twelve situations in which one power source (or perhaps two somewhat equal power sources) might be most effective. Check the box(es) of the power sources you believe most closely reflect each situation. Compare your answers with a classmate and discuss the reasons why you agree or disagree.

Situation	*Role Power*	*Personality Power*	*Knowledge Power*
1. Insubordination by an employee in a nuclear power plant	☐	☐	☐
2. Retraining an older employee to operate a new-generation computer	☐	☐	☐
3. Motivating a staff employee whose productivity has dropped dramatically	☐	☐	☐
4. Lowering the authority line on all subordinates because of infractions by a few	☐	☐	☐
5. President of United States giving a State of the Union address to Congress (and to the country, via television)	☐	☐	☐
6. Minister appearing before congregation to ask for financial pledges	☐	☐	☐
7. Manager using MRT to counsel a valued employee who has been acting hostile	☐	☐	☐
8. Announcing discovery of a theft ring and a plan to combat recurrence	☐	☐	☐
9. Selling the need for a new piece of technical equipment to your superiors	☐	☐	☐
10. Announcing a layoff in your organization	☐	☐	☐
11. College president appearing before faculty for the first time	☐	☐	☐
12. Police chief speaking before graduating class of police academy	☐	☐	☐

SUMMARY

* The sensitive application of MRT makes the addition of structure more acceptable to employees and followers.
* Without structure, discipline, and authority, organizations can quickly become ineffective.
* Whether a manager or leader, where you set your authority line is important; the way you maintain it is critical.
* A typical manager's power of influence usually is based on role power; a leader's profile often capitalizes on personality power and good use of knowledge power.
* Leaders frequently downplay their role power, using it as a power base, because they know the importance of maximizing other sources of power.
* Some managers don't develop their personality power.
* Some managers and leaders do not fully utilize their knowledge power.
* Leaders and managers can improve their power of influence in the way they "handle" power, realizing that followers, especially empowered followers, are their real power source.

Jane and Gloria are unlikely friends. Jane is a small, quiet, timid woman of 36 whose marriage has recently fallen apart. She has returned to college in an effort to find a career that will help her put her life back together. Gloria is a powerful personality who operates a successful health spa. They met when Jane joined Gloria's spa.

Case 11: Courage

One evening, after closing the club, Jane and Gloria stopped in a nearby coffee shop. Jane began to talk about Gloria's behavior that night.

"Gloria, I'm amazed at how you can stand up for yourself when somebody starts to get out of line. Like tonight, you really put that John Spencer in his place. How do you do that?"

"In my opinion, leadership is 90 percent guts. Every once in a while, I actually look for an opportunity to get tough. Afterward, things go better."

"I wish I were more like you," said Jane. "Frankly, I'll never be a leader—I just don't have the courage. I've been a follower all my life, so I guess I'll stay one."

Gloria responded: "Anybody can be a leader if they really want to. In fact, I'm looking for an assistant right now. If you let me train you, you can have the job. I can give you the confidence you need to step out and run things when I'm gone."

Do you believe Gloria can convert Jane into a leader? Or are some people born to be followers? Defend your position. (And then turn to the back of the book to read the authors' position.)

Case 12: Compatibility

Major Branden and Captain Guerro are attending the same military leadership seminar. Major Branden has almost thirty years of service. Captain Guerro has less than ten. They are discussing the issue of blending the Mutual Reward Theory and additional structure together.

"So far," says Major Branden, "I'm not impressed with the formula proposed by our instructor. I understand MRT, but I think it is a weak approach. If I start out with such a soft human relations approach and then suddenly add more discipline, I'll be in trouble. It's like trying to mix oil and water. I believe the rewards one can get in the military are self-evident. Can you imagine me sitting down with a corporal and asking what rewards she expects from me?"

"Yes, I can," replied Captain Guerro. "I think it would be a good investment of your time. You'd discover what rewards are required these days to build motivation. And I think you would learn a great deal about yourself."

"Okay. I might give it a try. But I still can't see how MRT and more structure go together. To me, they are just not compatible."

"On the contrary. In my opinion, the more you use MRT, the more structure your team will accept. You see, you start out on a human basis, and once your team knows that you will give them certain rewards, then they will accept discipline more readily. It's the combination that works. When you use MRT first, you set the stage for more structure, not the other way around."

Captain Guerro continues. "We surely do see things differently. I don't think of MRT as a weak approach; just good sense. As a leader, I have a contract with the people under my command. The better the contract, the better the relationship, and the better the relationship, the more I can expect from them under stress. I want them to accept my orders when they are necessary. That's why I use MRT."

Do you agree or disagree with Captain Guerro? Are MRT and structure more compatible in some environments than others? Do you agree that those leaders who do a good job with MRT will be able to apply more structure without getting resistance? Is it possible to be a compassionate leader in the modern military establishment? (Read the authors' reactions in the back of the book.)

Mark each statement True (T) or False (F).

_____ 1. The more MRT is used, the more structure subordinates will accept.

_____ 2. Structure and discipline without MRT can be counterproductive and even lead to lower productivity.

_____ 3. Role or position power is personality based.

_____ 4. Leaders, vs. managers, usually expand their use of role power and diminish their use of knowledge power.

_____ 5. Scientists make excellent leaders because they have exceptional knowledge power.

_____ 6. Overemphasis of one source of power and neglect of others can injure the leader's image.

_____ 7. For an authority line to be effective, both leaders and subordinates need to know how and where it is set.

_____ 8. All successful leaders demonstrate a certain degree of charisma.

_____ 9. Managers and leaders utilize personality power at the same level.

_____10. A leader's power of influence often results from providing structure and balancing the power sources.

Turn to the back of the book to check your answers.

TOTAL CORRECT _____

7 Make Better Decisions More Decisively

Not to decide is to decide.
Harvey Cox

7 Make Better Decisions More Decisively

LEADERS WELCOME DECISION MAKING AS AN OPPORTUNITY TO EXPRESS THEIR LEADERSHIP

A chartered plane, flying over dense jungle, crashes. Both pilots are killed. The forty passengers, unharmed but in shock, wonder how to get back to civilization. None of the passengers has had jungle survival training. Through the group process, they decide that their chances of survival will be greater if they stick together. Their first action is to choose a single, strong leader. What kind of a person should they choose?

Selecting a leader, assuming there is a choice, is not an easy task. There are many factors to consider; however, the most important personal quality of a good leader is the ability to make good decisions. Why? Because there usually are many issues to be resolved every day. For example, for the stranded passengers, their questions would include: Which direction should the party take? What about food and water? Shelter from the elements? Protection from jungle insects and animals? The moment a leader is chosen, he or she must make decisions quickly and with authority.

In any and all leader-follower situations, good decision making eventually surfaces as a characteristic followers value highly. Leaders say the same thing in many ways.

> "Poor decision making is the downfall of most leaders."

> "Decision making is a symbol of leadership."

> "It's not just making good decisions, it's making them with authority and decisiveness."

> "Making decisions is the most demanding thing I do."

> "I'm accepted as the leader of this organization because I have been able to take it in the right direction. They may not vote for me on a popularity basis, but they respect me as a decision maker. That is why I remain their leader."

Subordinates or the rank and file also agree that decision making should be an integral part of the Leadership Formula.

> "We are totally dependent on the quality of decisions made at the top. If they are bad, we all get hurt."

> "It is certainly easy to follow a leader with charisma, but if the leader doesn't make the right decisions, my job is on the line."

"You quickly lose respect for a leader who can't make good decisions. There is nothing more frustrating than having to work for someone who can't make up his or her mind."

When a coach makes superior decisions, players win games and feel good about their leadership. When a mayor makes good decisions, the quality of life in the city improves. When a corporate president makes the right decisions, everyone who works for the company benefits.

MAKING GOOD DECISIONS INCREASES YOUR FOLLOWERSHIP

Good decisions earn leaders the support of subordinates. Followers can and should contribute, where possible, to the decision-making process. Leaders who involve their employees in the process are aware of the rewards. And, if decision making can take place at the lowest level possible, two things happen: first, employees become empowered; and second, leaders can concentrate on the higher level decisions. Both employees and leaders (and the organization) are the winners.

Leaders, in the final analysis, must make the critical decisions. The burden is theirs. And our dependence on the decision-making ability of our leaders cannot be overestimated. For example, President Harry Truman was forced into making some tough decisions while in office. We are still living with the atomic bomb decision. It follows that the destiny of any group, organization, or country lies with the decisions made by its leader. There is no escape.

If you improve your decision making, you will increase your power of influence and your ability to effectively use the Mutual Reward Theory. As a result, you add more leadership to your management style.

IMPROVING YOUR DECISION MAKING PROCESS

Decision making has never been easy. It never will be. Leaders who can communicate well, use MRT sensitively, and exercise power wisely may ultimately fail because of poor decision making. Even those who are good at decision making will make a few bad decisions that come back to haunt them. No one is perfect.

How can you improve your propensity for making good decisions? If you will follow these three steps and then develop a process that fits your style and comfort zone, you will be well on your way to better decision making.

1. Sit down in a quiet place alone. Do not make major decisions on the run or under pressure.

2. Clear all distracting elements from your mind. Good decisions require concentration.

3. Devise a process similar to the one in the following exercise, "An Outline for Decision Making." Do not underestimate the importance of outlining (writing out) the process you will follow.

AN OUTLINE FOR DECISION MAKING

step-by-step outline shows how the decision-making process works. Read the entries under the column titled "Process." Note that there is one step for each letter representing the word DECISIONS. Then, read the entries under "Instructions." Follow the outline so you will be able to apply the process to any decision you make in the future.

Process	*Instructions*
Define desired outcome.	You need to know exactly what you want to accomplish before you can decide the best way to do it. As appropriate, get others involved in the process as early as possible.
Establish decision criteria.	What are the guideposts? (i.e., if you were deciding whether to drive or take the bus to work, you would consider factors like car wear and tear, safety, cost, and time saved.)
Consider the alternative solutions.	Write out all possible courses of action that will lead to the desired outcome. Involve others as appropriate (team discussion at this stage can be very beneficial).
Investigate—get all possible facts.	Accumulate as many facts as time permits. Again, followers can add significantly to fact finding. List the facts (pros and cons) for each possible solution.
Settle on top three choices.	List your choices; note the reasons for your three selections; then "sleep" on your choices going over the pros and cons (and your biases) of each.
Initiate a comparison of the choices.	Weigh your three choices; reevaluate the pros and cons (and your biases) to help you decide among them. Consult with others if necessary.
Opt for the best choice.	Write out your final decision; note the reason(s) for your choice. Keep your notes to compare with future decisions (you may have a decision-making "pattern" or style).
Notify those involved with decisiveness.	The way you articulate your decision can be as important as the quality of the decision itself. Write out how and to whom you will announce your decision.
See that decision is fully implemented.	A good decision must be made to work. Write out how you intend to put your decision into action. Take action (rate your "success" to compare with future decisions).

Do leaders actually follow models like the one illustrated each time they make a decision? Do they always stop, clear their minds, and then proceed, step by step, through a structured procedure? Of course not. (However, many have used a step-by-step outline for the purpose of improving their decision-making skills). While most successful leaders do not consciously use a check list for decision making, most rely heavily on some form of logical process and many make a flowchart of their plan of action even if it is brief. Following a logical process helps leaders make better decisions.

THE MORE LOGIC THE BETTER

Keep in mind that few leaders ever find a single procedure for decision making that is always reliable. Most experiment with a number of approaches, constantly attempting to improve their skills. Also, many good decision makers seem to select different procedures for different kinds of problems. For example, they might follow a structured pattern for a major problem, a more intuitive pattern for a minor one. Input from followers or turning the problem over to a team also can be an important element in the process—actually a decision in itself.

Sometimes time does not permit a formal step-by-step analysis of problem situations. As one manager stated,

> Despite all the computer data available to me, I still make lots of gut decisions. I just don't have time to gather and fully analyze all the facts. Things are moving too fast. There are too many emergencies.

But every leader should, when possible, follow a logical pattern to improve the quality of decisions (You may wish to refer back to the exercise, An Outline for Decision Making, as one example). Leaders who follow logic reduce the risk of making bad decisions. Our outline for decision making shows what some experts might consider an ideal process under ideal conditions. You may never find an "ideal condition," but eventually you need to develop a process that works for you. Finding one "best" method of decision making may be, as most leaders claim, a never-ending search that will always require adjustments and improvements to fit the situation. But the effort must be made.

It stands to reason that clear thinking is required for good decision making. A muddled mind will not make a clear decision. For many decision makers, time and place play a critical role in promoting clear thinking. Some people believe they think more clearly early in the morning, after a good night's sleep and before the daily pressures pile up. Others say that they must get away to another environment to sort things out more clearly. A growing number of executives claim that jogging, running, or other forms of physical exercise produce a "clarity of thinking" that help them make better decisions. Each individual needs to experience many decision-making climates to discover the one or two that work best.

CLARITY OF THINKING

Obviously, anything a decision maker can do to clear his or her head for thinking is worth doing.

INDECISION IS A BAD DECISION

Leaders must be careful not to spend so much of their time perfecting their decision-making model that they cannot provide direction when it is needed. When there is indecision, organizations become fragmented and employees scramble in different directions. A case in point:

> Everyone had high hopes for the new university president. He was a disciplined academician, an accomplished writer, a good communicator, and an outstanding manager. But it soon became apparent that he could not make hard decisions quickly. In fact, the backlog of problems requiring major decisions nearly brought the university to a standstill. For example, in a time of increasing enrollments, he refused to trim the fat from his administrative staff and hire more teaching faculty, which resulted in heavier classroom loads for his already overburdened teaching staff. The issue of teaching eventually caused a faculty rebellion. Even before his four-year appointment was up, the board bought out his contract to avoid letting the university become totally ineffective.

Indecision in itself can be a decision—usually a bad one. And most followers want a leader who acts, even if a few mistakes are made along the way. Good leaders do not shirk their decision-making responsibility. Inaction and sweeping problems under the rug are not leadership qualities. Leaders cannot abdicate their leadership role. Good or bad, decisions must be made.

Not only should decisions be made within a reasonable length of time, they should be made with decisiveness. A decision, no matter how small it may be, should show the presence of leadership.

Perceptive leaders capitalize on opportunities to announce decisions they feel are particularly good. You hear them saying something to this effect: "I am proud to make this important announcement. This decision takes our organization in the right direction. All of us will come out ahead."

In announcing a decision, leaders should use their role power to set the stage and gain the attention of followers, their personality power to present the decision in the best light, and their knowledge power to communicate why the decision is a good one, based upon the facts.

Despite the fact that the rank and file may not always appear interested in the decisions their leaders make, there is a high correlation between the ability to make decisions and the image a leader projects. Here's an example:

> Greg made a hard decision when three of his key soccer players were found to be using drugs. They were suspended from the team for the season. A tough decision, but the rest of the players, as well as school officials, recognized it as the right one. Although they lost the next few games, the team still made it to the playoffs. The following year Greg discovered he had more support from players, administrators, and parents than ever before. His image had been enhanced.

> Victoria, who was the city's recreation director, recommended closing the downtown swimming pool when it became obvious there was not enough money to keep all three city pools open. Besides, she argued, the downtown pool, which was used primarily by poor minorities, was taking more of the city's resources than the other pools. Victoria underestimated the reaction from the community, and within ten days she had to withdraw her recommendation. As a result of her ill-advised decision, her image was damaged, and she knew it.

DECISION MAKING AND IMAGE

When a leader makes a decision to which most people will react positively, he or she should see that the message is widely broadcast. It can only enhance the leader's image. On the other hand, if an unpopular decision must be made, it should be soft-pedaled. When a leader makes a bad decision (and discovers it in time), she or he can only hope that it will not receive too much publicity—assuming, of course, that the leader has some control over the media. Media control, these days, is rather rare even for the most powerful leaders. Thus, a leader who thinks his or her media influence will carry her or him through a tough situation may be headed for a quick exit from a leadership position. When leaders in the public sector make serious mistakes, the prying eye of the media will generally uncover them. Sometimes public reaction can destroy even the most effective leader.

All leaders wind up making a bad decision now and then, and generally everybody finds out about it. It is usually the way in which leaders live with bad decisions that determines their real leadership capabilities. Those who quickly admit they made a mistake—before damage control gets out

LIVING WITH A BAD DECISION

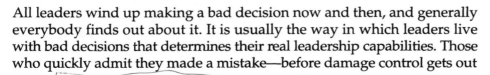

of control— and openly attempt to take direct, corrective action to repair the damage usually come out ahead. Consider the following examples of the way bad decisions were handled by Helen and Raymond.

> Helen, the training director for a large corporation, found that a few employees signed up for training courses and were given credit for courses they did not attend. She made the decision to keep the discovery to herself, but made sure the practice was stopped immediately. Later, because of a company promotion policy, it all came out. Helen quickly admitted she had made the wrong decision and apologized openly to the entire company. She made no further attempts to cover up, but training no longer carried the prestigious place in the organization it previously had enjoyed. The administration did not remove Helen from her position; however, some damage was done to her image. It took a long time for her to build up overall confidence in the training program, but the program survived. She developed better program procedures and tighter controls; and, in the end, she wound up with a little more stature (with most people) than she had before.

> Raymond knew he made a mistake the second day after he appointed Rick as his assistant. Rick did nothing but rub everyone the wrong way. Productivity slumped. Morale quickly went down. How did Raymond react? He lost confidence in his ability to make good decisions, and things went from bad to worse. When it was all over, and Raymond had resigned, he decided he did not want to have anything to do with any kind of leadership role in the future. Decision making was not his cup of tea.

It is not easy to live with a bad decision. It can destroy confidence and cause the decision maker to be indecisive in the future. Additionally, it can undermine anyone's faith in his or her own ability to make good decisions.

But, a few bad decisions do not a poor leader make. A leader's overall image counts more than his or her won/lost record. And one way to compensate for a bad decision is to quickly make good decisions that neutralize or offset the bad one.

REVERSING BAD DECISIONS

Reversing a bad decision is common, yet a decision reversal often has less impact upon the leader's image than one might expect. Many leaders have reported that they lose far less respect when they openly reverse a bad decision than when they let it simmer. While subordinates may have a higher tolerance for bad decisions than most people suspect, the rank and file have a tendency to pick apart even the best decision. We are in a time in society when negativism runs high—partly because company loyalty to its employees (and, in return, employee loyalty to the organization) has diminished so much.

Leaders, however, know they will receive criticism. They must rise above negativity, keep a positive attitude, and do what is best for the organization. For this reason, good leaders know it is still better to reverse a bad decision, rather than leave it—and to reverse it quickly. Consider the following quotation:

> I believe most followers view their leaders as they do their favorite baseball players. They do not expect their leaders to bat 1000 on decision making. Not that they don't hold their leaders accountable, they do; but they don't expect the impossible.

Decision making may be a primary criterion for superior leadership, but no one expects miracles. People want clear decisions; they want quick decisions; and they want decisions that are good for the organization and themselves. And if a bad decision is made, they want their leaders to acknowledge their part in it and then do something about it before anyone is hurt even more. A reversal is far more acceptable than a bad decision that is allowed to remain in force.

A leader who makes a serious mistake and then corrects it is forgiven. But the leader who reverses a decision because of pressure from special-interest groups is respected by no one. It is true that the best decision is the one that benefits everyone, but even when it is impossible to please all subgroups, a decision must be made. Once the best decision has been made, it is wise to stick with it even though not everyone is happy. Leaders who permit pressure from one group to cause them to flip-flop on a decision usually wind up making everyone unhappy.

DECISION FLIP-FLOPS DESTROY LEADERSHIP IMAGE

DECISION MAKING AND THE GROUP PROCESS

Most organizations understand the power of teamwork. Many have strengthened themselves by taking the time to involve employees in those decisions that affect them the most—in the decisions of the organization's day-to-day operations. Employees gain ego satisfaction from being involved and are more apt to be enthusiastic about decisions in which they have participated. Satisfaction is translated into work contributions which result in higher productivity. There is a purpose and they are all pulling together toward a common goal. Morale improves. The Mutual Reward Theory is in motion and the leader's effectiveness is increased.

The leader who empowers workers in company decision making, and, as a result, increases the followers' as well as his or her own contributions to the company goals, is a valuable asset to any organization. There are many decision-making situations where involving subordinates is especially wise—when more information is needed to make a good decision, when it is necessary to eliminate resistance to whatever the ultimate decision will be, and when a team can contribute much more than the sum of individual efforts (which is a reality in most businesses today).

Leaders who surround themselves with competent people are making an investment in their own leadership success. That is, by empowering followers and helping them improve their decision-making skills, leaders increase their own decision-making capability. Leaders also are able to give more attention to the critical issues and higher-level decisions that drive the very essence of the company's existence.

There are, however, some dangers of rank-and-file involvement in decision making. It is the leader's responsibility to determine when their participation may outweigh the advantages. For example, if the process takes too long, the decision may be delayed and the leader accused of indecisiveness. Another danger is involving some subordinates and not others, creating dissension and divisiveness in the ranks. Additionally, the group could come up with a team decision that is so full of compromises that the decision is less effective than the one the leader could have made alone.

To avoid the pitfalls of group decision making, the leader must become adept at knowing when and when not to delegate decisions—a decision in itself. The leader also must become very good at knowing when and how much authority and responsibility should be given to a team in the decision-making process. The balance is critical; learning the right balance is an evolutionary process. It takes time and practice by the leader.

If the leader loses his or her ability to control team decision making (that is, the leader gives away too much authority to the team), the leader may end up in a no-win situation. The leader who is "forced" either to go along with the decision or to override it has given away too much authority with the decision-making process. The line of authority is not clear to all involved. And, if the leader overrides the decision, the problems that result will probably be much greater than those created by living with it. The end result usually is that the leader loses or diminishes her or his power of influence.

Time permitting, democratic decision making can produce outstanding results. In many situations, team decision making is the best approach to take. On the other hand, too much consultation can communicate leadership weakness. The right balance is possible but is hard to achieve.

In weighing all the factors that go into a leader's decision-making ability, one of the most critical is selecting his or her immediate or inner circle of staff. Choosing the wrong staff member has caused the downfall of more leaders than any other single factor. Because selecting staff is extremely important to a leader, the more often a leader needs to add a new staff member or replace an old one, the more chance there is to make a mistake.

SELECTION OF STAFF: A CRITICAL DECISION

Why is it so difficult to select enthusiastic, capable, loyal staff members? The primary reason appears to lie in the premise that a leader needs staff members who are a reflection of his or her leadership style. In other words, when you ask someone to be a member of your inner circle, you are, in effect, saying: "I am asking you, as a staff member and follower, to support my policies and leadership style so that we can present a united front and image to outside followers. Within our circle, we can express our differences openly. In return, I will do my best to provide you with all rewards, both personal and professional."

Trouble often seems to start with a difference in opinion based upon a conflicting set of values. But the root of the problem is apt to be a difference in style. When a leader can no longer feel comfortable with a subordinate in a staff role, time seldom produces a solution. The same is true if the subordinate is not happy with the leader's style. The best thing for both parties is for the staff member to resign; the worst thing is for the staff member to initiate critical infighting and, eventually, become disloyal.

Leaders often seem to have blind spots in selecting their staff. Why? Perhaps they project their own image into the behavior of another; perhaps they see only what they want to see; perhaps they fail to employ the process and skills they would normally use in other types of decisions. No leader can be expected to make perfect staff selections all the time—after all, it is hard to predict how the selected person will perform under the leader's direction. That is, a person might perform quite differently under the new leader than that person did in a previous position.

A number of factors may enter into how a person performs under a new leader—new environment, new management style, new responsibilities and pressures, new coworkers and subordinates, etc. The leader assumes considerable risk in selecting staff members. Here are three suggestions that could improve the staff-selection process for some leaders.

1. *Get the opinions of others.* Few leaders have had extensive personnel and interviewing experience; so they, more than others, need professional advice in this area. Leaders should seek honest opinions from objective people (those already onboard), listen carefully, and then make a decision. The selection process is one that should not be rushed—if at all possible.

2. *Discuss your leadership style with candidates.* Explain why you need staff members who will be an extension of your style and not their own. Admit that there is a "conformity price" to be paid as far as projecting an external image is concerned. Then discuss the advantages and how MRT can apply. Give an applicant time to assess your invitation.

3. *Interview at least three applicants.* Your interviews with at least three potential candidates should be thorough and in-depth. Complete your research on each person before you extend an invitation to join your staff. Satisfy yourself that the individual you selected will become a team member and contribute to the productivity, enthusiasm, and enjoyment of other staff members.

Leaders frequently find that even after they have taken careful precautions to select the right staff for their team, a mistake can still be made. When this happens, take immediate action to remedy the situation. "Better now than later" is a good motto to follow if a staff member doesn't seem to be working out. Follow all the principles of MRT, the law, and recognized procedures—but act. Your future role as a leader will depend upon it!

Confidence and leadership are first cousins. Insecure people who are always looking for ways to protect themselves, or who prefer to stay out of the limelight, do not become good leaders. On the other hand, taking the limelight at the expense of other people—that is, taking credit for something that should be given to others—equally is not a good leadership characteristic. Those people who will do anything to keep people liking them do not become effective leaders. And people who avoid controversy at all costs will not enjoy long-term leadership.

CONFIDENCE AND DECISION MAKING

Confidence or courage means taking a stand that may not be popular but is best for the group. It means making a tough decision, knowing you might be proved wrong at a later date. It means saying "no" to someone you like, knowing that she or he may turn against you in the future. It means risking rejection by people for whom you care just because you must make an unpopular decision.

Generally speaking, people who postpone making a difficult decision do so because they lack the courage or confidence to make it. Those who form committees and ask for recommendations (when they already have the facts) are often delaying decisions to get themselves off the hook. All leaders must make some hard decisions and making them usually takes guts. There is no escape.

Leaders recognize that some isolation from their subordinates, even members of their staff, is part of the role they play. (It is indeed often lonely at the top.) Strong emotional stability is a quality leaders must have to do their jobs effectively on a day-to-day basis. A positive attitude is central to your emotional stability. A leader's positive attitude and reliance on his or her own strengths and resources may be very significant to get her or him through a crisis or critical situation.

EMOTIONAL STRENGTH— A NECESSITY

Leaders who have emotional strength stay calm in turmoil. They handle stress without becoming too discouraged. They handle outside criticism without taking it too personally. Only subordinates enjoy the luxury of relaxing under the protective umbrella of the organization; they can, for the most part, exempt themselves from the organizational stress and pressure felt by those "at the top."

Leaders cannot become part of the crowd. They must take the punches as they come. They cannot develop a defeatist attitude when something goes wrong or a bad decision has been made; they must bounce back—quickly. They must live through traumatic bad decision reversals, but strive to minimize them. They must accept the fact that leaders are not always popular. They must learn to live with the fact that both their actions and their words will sometimes be misinterpreted.

STAGING DECISION ANNOUNCEMENTS

Have you noticed how political and corporate leaders use the media to stage announcements of major decisions? Even in much smaller ways (and probably without media help), staging major announcements is a good idea for all leaders. Here's why.

1. Followers who hear about a decision affecting them and who hear it directly from the leader are apt to support it. Often, support is even better if the announcement is made with fanfare and decisiveness.

2. The sooner followers know about a decision that impacts them, the better. Even positive whispers through a grapevine or rumormill can distort good intentions. Delays can cause irreparable damage.

3. A well-staged announcement becomes a positive force and can enhance your leadership image. Followers need to see, hear, and react in a positive way to the leaders who have a strong power of influence.

While only a small percentage of leaders may have mass media access, whatever your position, do everything you can to stage the announcement of a major decision. Have your staff set the stage, try for the largest audience, and use your best platform manner and presentation skills to deliver a positive announcement. Use all the showmanship possible, as long as it falls within your comfort zone.

The rewards of good decision making are immeasurable. And, putting more leadership into your style through better, sharper decision making depends on you—it is a do-it-yourself project. The effort you make to improve your decisiveness is worth it. Success will earn you greater respect from those who are dependent upon your leadership, because good decision making is tantamount to a reward they will appreciate. Good decisions will either keep you in your leadership role or open the door to a better one!

DECISION-MAKING REWARDS

* Leaders and followers agree that good decision making is a primary criterion for successful leadership.
* Most people can improve their decision-making skills by a system or procedure that employs logic. However, a procedure can only lead to a better decision; it cannot make it.
* Leaders are respected when they make the best decision in a quick, decisive manner.
* Selecting staff and making personnel decisions can be very difficult; they are very critical decisions for a leader.
* Leadership is often signaled as much by the way a decision is announced as by the decision itself.
* There is a high correlation between good decision making and the kind of leadership image that is signaled.
* The group decision-making process should be followed; its purpose is to empower followers and lead to good decisions.
* It is better to correct a bad decision—quickly—than to live with it.
* Wherever possible, major decisions should be staged or dramatized to reinforce their potential impact.

SUMMARY

Case 13: Viewpoint

Al Bello is a paid leader for a fund-raising, charity organization. Jessica James is the owner of her own business. They are good friends and frequently get together to discuss their successes and failures. "I've been agonizing over my decisions for over twenty years," claims Al Bello, "and frankly, I believe I should have devoted more time to announcing and articulating my decisions and less time to making them. I believe you can make a so-so decision and, providing you announce it with decisiveness, conviction, and strength, it may accomplish more than a better decision announced in a more routine manner. Does this make sense?"

"I agree," Jessica replied, "that announcing and articulating a decision in a forceful manner is important, but nothing can take away the sting of a bad decision, or even a poor one. Sooner or later the quality of your decisions will catch up to you. My decisions are designed to keep my company in a profit mode so that my employees will continue to work enthusiastically. If I make a decision that disrupts that pattern, I'm in trouble, no matter how much attention and power I put behind the announcement."

"I'm not so sure the quality of one's decisions means that much," stated Al. "There is a time-lag element. By the time those involved can tell whether a good or bad decision has been made, they have forgotten who made it. Or they don't care. In the future, I'm going to make the best possible decision without spending so much time in reaching the decision and then spend more time implementing it. If my subordinates think I am a good leader, they will go along with my decisions, good or bad. We should use decisions to communicate our leadership, not our logic."

"I can't follow your rationale on this," Jessica responded. "You are a good leader if you make good decisions. This is true because you are leading in the right direction. The fact that others may not know you are making sound decisions is not as important as your knowing it. And, besides, sooner or later all decisions come back to haunt you. I know."

Which viewpoint would you support? Is there such a thing as a decision time lag? Do we hold our leaders responsible for their decisions? Is the decision-making process overestimated as a leadership essential? (The authors' comments are given in the back of the book.)

Members of the board of trustees for a small, private foundation are writing the criteria for the selection of a new chief financial officer. The previous CFO left the organization in a state of chaos because of a series of poor decisions.

Three board members agree that it would be a good idea for anyone submitting an application to also submit a decision-making track record. The record would include a list of major decisions over the past five years, the applicant's assessment of why they were good decisions, and verification from a responsible party that the decisions turned out well for all concerned. Anyone who did not submit such a record would not be considered.

The remaining two trustees take an opposing view. They believe it is impossible to verify whether a decision is good or bad. They feel many highly qualified leaders would not submit applications because of this requirement. Further, they feel it is virtually impossible to determine ahead of time the decision-making capabilities of an applicant.

Which group would you support? What suggestion might you make to help them select a good decision maker without having each applicant submit a record? Do you feel the board is placing too much emphasis on decision making to the detriment of more important characteristics? (Turn to the back of the book to read the authors' opinions.)

Self-Test

Mark each statement True (T) or False (F).

_____ 1. Improving your decision-making ability is a good way to put more leadership into your style.

_____ 2. The way you announce and articulate a decision has little to do with the leadership image you communicate.

_____ 3. Leaders welcome decision making as a way to express their leadership.

_____ 4. Good decision makers always follow the same logical, prescribed procedure.

_____ 5. It is best to acknowledge bad decisions and take immediate corrective action.

_____ 6. Following a standard decision-making process for thirty days can improve the quality of decisions for the inexperienced leader.

_____ 7. The team or group process of decision making empowers followers and invariably produces better and faster decisions.

_____ 8. A poor decision, made with decisiveness, can be better than no decision at all.

_____ 9. Decision making does not bother leaders as much as followers.

_____10. There is no such thing as a "gut decision."

Turn to the back of the book to check your answers.

TOTAL CORRECT_____

8 Strive to Become a Visionary

It is a time for a new generation of leadership to cope with new problems and new opportunities. For there is a new world to be won.

John F. Kennedy

8 Strive to Become a Visionary

LEADERS CREATE AND ARTICULATE A MISSION TO THEIR FOLLOWERS

You have now reached a point in the book where the following emphatic statements have true meaning: Effective communication is vital to star leadership! Leaders have a responsibility to help employees become empowered followers! Leaders find ways to expand their power of influence! Leaders make decisions in a decisive manner!

These four critical and interrelated leadership characteristics are represented in the Leadership Formula and illustrated by a star in the Leadership Strategic Model (Chapter 3). In addition to these four elements, our leadership star model also places another element—vision—at the pinnacle of the star. That is, leaders must provide direction or vision; they must lead toward something of meaning and significance. A potential victory must be provided somewhere down the road. Here's a case in point.

> On a flight to Washington, D.C., a woman executive was seated by a young Native American who was flying to the capital to accept a Small Business Administration award for starting a successful business to recycle steel slag. The two individuals had a good conversation, touching on many subjects. The executive was most impressed, however, by the way in which the young man interpreted the mission of his small company. "Our purpose is to live in harmony with the land—to use what we take, to return what we do not need. It is the Indian way."

The young man obviously knew exactly how to articulate his company's mission and, in turn, his company's goals. That is, his company's goals were to do the tasks and operations that were necessary to make money and survive—he was being honored for his business success. He was also being honored for his "visionary" success—the conservation of natural resources. His vision or company mission made him stand out as a leader who had a business plan to accomplish great things.

Peter Drucker, in his book *Managing for Results,** discusses the importance of a single organizational goal for managers and employees. It follows that, if such a goal exists (and is articulated), the goal could and should be converted into a mission. Peter Drucker also points out in *Post-Capitalist Society,*† that a "prerequisite of an organization's performance" must be a crystal clear task and mission (p. 55).

*New York, Harper & Row, 1964.
† New York, HarperCollins Publishers, 1993.

When an organization fails to see or articulate its vision to employees, workers may see their role in the company merely as going to work, doing what they are told, going home, and repeating the scenario again the next day. Most people find little satisfaction in a routine without a purpose, even though a paycheck at regular intervals is a reward.

Most people underestimate their need (and that of others) to have a high vision or dream on the horizon. The majority of managers fall into this category. So do some leaders. The lack of a mission is the reason many organizations falter. It is also the reason why work is nothing but work for most people.

NEED FOR A BIGGER VISION

A mission has three main purposes which apply to both managers and employees:

MISSION:
1. A mission gives the whole organization a sense of unity and purpose.
2. A mission provides the focus for everyone to move in the same direction.
3. A mission is a motivator.

A mission, especially one that is well articulated, provides a positive force for action for everyone. Leaders with a vision or mission can motivate people to action, empower them with responsibility for their actions, and reward them accordingly. In turn, motivated, empowered followers enhance a leader's image and power of influence. Everyone comes out a winner.

Sad though it is to acknowledge, individual productivity in America (taking into consideration the technological conditions at the time) was never greater than during World War II. Why? Because almost everyone had a mission. People wanted to be part of a victory that was over the horizon. Victory in itself became a mission. While peacetime missions may be less inspirational, the possibility of inspiration still exists in all situations where individuals operate as a group or team.

True leaders acknowledge with enthusiasm that humankind does not live or work for bread alone (neither dollars nor subsistence). Most people will tell you that while a paycheck usually is critical, work satisfaction is very important to them. Leaders, too, know that employees want something beyond dollars, benefits, security, promotions, recognition, and the promise of retirement. They want to be a part of something bigger than themselves—and the key word is *part*. Workers become followers when they become part of an effort—a feeling of worth—that has real significance. They feel differently when they are part of a movement or team. It is not just little personal victories that most employees seek; rather, they want to participate, share in decision making, and celebrate group victory. Being part of an effort makes the employees interested in the company's mission. They become stakeholders in results and outcomes. As stakeholders they take interest in the company versus just doing a day's work.

A VISIONARY VS. A GOAL SETTER

If you first understand the basic difference between a visionary and a goal setter, it becomes clear why many leaders are "visionary goal setters."

> A visionary is
> one whose ideas and plans are not always practical.
> A goal setter is
> one who makes practical goals exciting and reachable.

A leader who is a visionary goal setter can articulate a vision or dream and back it up with small, reachable goals that, once achieved, provide victories along the way. Whether the vision ever materializes may not be important, as long as it provides direction and supplements the motivation to reach the goals.

A mission can be a rainbow in the sky; a goal can be a task or a chore. A mission can be a dream or a vision; a goal can be a duty one is expected to perform. A mission provides meaning and self-fulfillment; a goal provides rewards that may be soon forgotten. Generally, a goal is more immediate, more pragmatic, and more mundane than a mission.

> A goal, by definition, must be reachable;
> a mission need not.
> A mission does not have to be accomplished—and may never be;
> but it must stir the imagination and feed the soul.

Many people complain that they do not feel good about the work they are doing. There is little personal gratification, little recognition, or little glory. Perhaps it is because their leaders have not provided a sense of mission that would give their efforts meaning. The leader who can create and articulate such a mission will always have followers. The two examples that follow show some of the main differences between missions and goals:

Let's say that two entrepreneurs, Harvey and Tran, started similar businesses at the same time under similar conditions. Harvey's goal was to show a profit after two years and then double it annually for the following three years. Tran's goal was to create a model or prototype business that would attract national attention; and, as a result, could be franchised across the country. Those in the "start-up operation" would be furnished key franchise opportunities (at minimum cost) ahead of outsiders.

Although both entrepreneurs had a goal, Tran also had a vision. Tran could picture a model operation that was so good others would want to copy it, and soon it would be copied throughout the country. The difference is significant. Perhaps Harvey wanted to be a profitable owner/manager, whereas Tran wanted to be a leader in the industry.

Here's a second example:

A successful developer/builder conceived of a retirement center that would be a showcase for the region. The center would be elegant but affordable, safe and secure, close to community activities, functional but not crowded. He and a staff of architects spent three years on the design. Once the property was acquired, he conducted a series of meetings for staff, subcontractors, community leaders, and others concerned with the development. At each meeting he carefully painted a vision—his dream of providing quality living for the elderly and showcasing the results for the region.

As the massive center was built and developed step by step, the developer/builder continued to keep his dream alive. He utilized and capitalized on several forms of communication to talk about and promote his dream. On the job site, he praised the good work of construction workers. He discussed the center's qualities with potential inhabitants. And he used the media to reach beyond the local community into the surrounding area to showcase the complex.

For his efforts, he won the support and backing of a great number of people. Once the retirement center was completed, no one was surprised that he received so many favorable compliments from community leaders for his contribution and the high level of productivity achieved by everyone involved.

Although not true in all cases, managers are apt to settle for immediate productivity goals, without creating a vision first. Leaders, on the other hand, are apt to start with an exciting, imaginative vision to capture minds and enthusiasm, then supplement the dream with immediate goals. Leaders appeal to pride and fulfillment; they attempt to make followers feel important by providing them with the opportunity to share in a victory that is bigger than themselves.

LEADERS SUPPORT THE NEED FOR MISSION

It is not an accident that the topmost point in the leadership star (Leadership Strategic Model) represents the need for a vision, mission, or overriding purpose. The leaders in the original survey which formed the basis of this book insisted on it. All enthusiastically supported the need to have and articulate something beyond typical goals. It is becoming increasingly important, especially for an organization to be successful, to have a well-articulated mission.

For most leaders,
a mission is
the essence of leadership.

Creating the right mission and then articulating it is a major challenge. Here are some successful leaders' comments that suggest both their enthusiasm for the idea (vision or mission) and their struggles to make it work:

"Any leadership concept that does not include the responsibility of creating an overall purpose or vision is shallow indeed."

"The purpose of a mission is to provide direction, and direction is what leadership is all about."

"The most important thing a mission does is motivate the leader."

CONVERTING A PRIMARY GOAL INTO A MISSION

Sometimes a goal can be converted into a mission by following a procedure like this:

1. Isolate the three most important goals within the group or organization;

2. Select the one that has the greatest appeal;

3. Convert this goal into a mission by giving it a broader perspective— less task oriented, more encompassing, greater depth and breadth, and, in general, more global in scope (a dynamic title also may add to the conversion); and

4. Articulate the mission in such a way that it stands above organizational goals.

Another way to come up with a suitable mission is through the technique of brainstorming. Brainstorming should not be limited by barriers such as negative feedback. To explain: When a leader gathers a group of people together, they might brainstorm a broad question such as "What are we really trying to do here?" Group members are asked to offer suggestions to answer the question.

The ground rules of true brainstorming dictate that there are no right or wrong answers. One person should not "put down" another's suggestion, only add to it. Statements like "No, that won't work because . . ." should not be allowed in the initial stage of brainstorming. Why? Because negativism and barriers need to be put aside to promote creative thinking and idea generation. Once ideas are generated, each one can be discussed and their merits weighed, pro and con.

Often a mission will surface in the first group brainstorming session mainly because people are excited about being involved in the process. The group technique also makes sense because those who will carry out the mission should, if possible, be involved in creating it. If a mission statement doesn't stir their imaginations or give them a sense of pride, it is probably the wrong mission for that group. Of course, it is also important that the leader be committed to the mission. A good mission is often an extension of the leader—an integral part of his or her leadership style and power of influence.

WINNING IS AN ACCEPTABLE MISSION

It is not always possible for a leader to create an ideal or original mission. But even if a leader can't create one that inspires or excites, all is not lost. The sense of pride that accompanies winning can be a good mission. Sometimes there is no need to look further. In this respect, coaches have a big advantage over other leaders. They have an inherent, automatic mission—winning! And best of all, every time they start a new season, their sense of mission is renewed.

Winning is upbeat, exciting, and full of personal rewards. If you have ever participated in a sport, you may know the pride that comes from playing on a winning team. There is nothing quite like it. But teams are not the only organizations that win. It is a great feeling to be with a business organization that is making a profit and expanding (winning). It is a great feeling to work for an educational institution that has high standards and successful programs (winning); it is a great feeling to be on a police force that is admired and respected by the community it serves (winning).

Any type or size of organization or group can be a winner. And winning comes in many different ways, shapes, quantities, etc., to compliment a situation. Leaders, in practicing the Mutual Reward Theory, are adept at promoting a winning atmosphere. Leaders promote a winning environment by assuring the mission is very clear and well articulated to everyone. They value, recognize, and reward good work. In essence, they focus on rewarding performance toward furthering the company's overarching mission. And they promote the goals that will mobilize the organization's strategic plan to get there.

OTHER QUALITIES FOR BECOMING A VISIONARY

Developing good mission statements and becoming a visionary are lofty aspirations for anyone. And if you think that you must be born a visionary to be one, you are wrong. You can always increase your propensity to become better at nearly everything if you try. You can always learn new ways of doing things and benefit from skill practice and character development. Thus, it is a moot point that to be a visionary, one must be born a visionary* or have a special gift. All others are not left out. One just needs to look for opportunities and challenges. As Gareth Morgan puts it in his book, *Imagin-i-zation: New Mindsets for Seeing, Organizing, and Managing,*[†] "the challenge now is to imaginize . . . to develop fresh ways of thinking about yourself and your organization . . . and . . . to organize for flexibility and innovation." (p.xxix)

Most people who carefully study management principles and leadership styles agree that there are numerous skills that enhance a person's ability to be successful managers and leaders. And leaders themselves know it is to their advantage to build (and strengthen) their knowledge, skills, and personal characteristics.

Here are several characteristics and skills that most successful leaders agree need to be developed to their fullest: positive attitude, thinking and decision making, creativity, imagination, innovativeness, flexibility, accepting and adapting to change, researching and exploring new insights, attacking problems as challenges, mobilizing ideas, and rethinking (reimaging, reinventing, reinterpreting, reenhancing, reengineering, etc.) everything.

No doubt, these characteristics and skills are also the attributes that should be high on your list. In the book, *The Tom Peters Seminar: Crazy Times Call for Crazy Organizations,*[‡] Tom Peters quotes a MCI middle manager as saying, "Do something. Make things happen. It's inaction that kills you." (p112)

Taking decisive action toward a goal of improving your skills is good advice. If you desire to become a visionary, it will take effort and practice. But if you make a conscious effort to improve those characteristics and skills you admire in successful leaders, you will undoubtedly join the winner's circle.

Winning is gratifying for anyone. And one of the best ways to make strides in the right direction toward the winner's circle is to expand your horizons. Reading will do that. Read everything, not just material in your area of interest. Reading is one of the best ways to expand your interests and creative thought. As you increase your knowledge base by reading, you will begin to think of things in new ways. You will begin to challenge yourself. And, as you do, you start "coloring outside the lines."

---

*A case in point is the long-standing debate of whether or not managers are born (natural talent) or made (learned or acquired) and whether or not management is a science or an art. The fact that there are so many formal programs focused on managerial and leadership development should provide some food for thought for those who still wish to debate the subject.

[†]*San Francisco, CA: Berrett-Koehler Pub., Inc.; and Thousand Oaks, CA: Sage Pub., Inc., 1997.*

[‡]*Excel/A California Partnership, 1994 (New York: Random House, Vintage Books).*

COLOR OUTSIDE THE LINES

Complete the following creative thinking exercise by writing the name of something that is a circle or represents a circle in each of the 12 circles below. Time yourself to see how long it takes you to complete the exercise. Note the time.

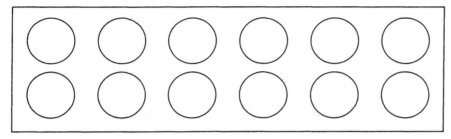

_____Total time (first attempt)

Before you do the exercise a second time, think of "families" of circular things. For example, how many wheels or planets can you name? Now, try the exercise a second time. Note the time.

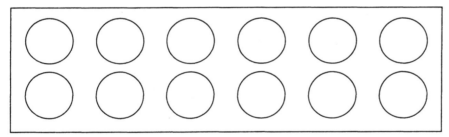

_____Total time (second attempt)

Compare your time in your first round with your time in the second round. In the second round, were you able to complete the exercise in less (maybe considerably less) time? Draw some conclusions about yourself and the way you approached the exercise. What additional ways can you think of to complete the exercise—to tax your imagination and expand your creative thinking skills?

If you expect to excel at developing mission statements, you probably will need to practice your skill in writing good statements. On the following page you will find an exercise to test your ability to write three mission statements. Before you do the exercise, however, consider the

DEVELOPING MISSION STATEMENTS

following ten questions that can lead to the development of a strong mission statement. A good mission statement does not necessarily include every one of the ten points; however, these questions can be used as guidelines to follow in developing your mission-writing skills. Remember, you need not occupy a management or leadership role to begin honing your skills in writing mission statements. As you practice, keep a positive attitude. Also, keep in mind that leaders who create their own missions are usually enthusiastic about them.

10 QUESTIONS TO ADDRESS WHEN DEVELOPING MISSION STATEMENTS

Read the following questions before writing the three mission statements explained in the next exercise, "Writing Mission Statements."

Once you have written your three mission statements, measure each against the ten questions below. A "Yes" response to the majority of questions indicates you appear to be on the right track in writing good mission statements.

		Yes	No
1.	Does this mission lead everyone in the group in the best possible direction?	☐	☐
2.	Will it benefit all members equally?	☐	☐
3.	Will it help to sustain and protect the organization over the long term?	☐	☐
4.	Can I, as a leader, articulate the mission clearly to all members of the group?	☐	☐
5.	Can the mission be expressed as a slogan?	☐	☐
6.	Will the members of my group accept the mission with enthusiasm?	☐	☐
7.	Am I highly enthusiastic about it myself?	☐	☐
8.	Will the mission increase motivation appreciably?	☐	☐
9.	Is it sufficiently visionary to work?	☐	☐
10.	Is it the best mission under the circumstances?	☐	☐

WRITING MISSION STATEMENTS

Create a mission statement for each of the following three situations. When you are finished, measure each against the 10 questions above. Then, compare your statements with your classmates. Discuss the factors that will lead to a strong(er) mission statement for each situation.

You are the director of fund raising for a private ecology foundation. Your goal is to raise $10 million, a 20 percent jump over last year. Write a mission statement to implement your campaign.

_____

_____

You are a high school coach. Your goal is to be conference champion. Write a mission statement that will contribute to your goal.

_____

_____

As corporate president, you are seeking a mission statement that will improve the image of your organization as well as contribute to higher profits. Write a strong mission statement.

_____

_____

ARTICULATION

Many leaders forget that it is as important to articulate a mission as to create one. They assume that if the mission is a good one it will survive on its own. They are wrong. A mission, to be successful, must be transmitted clearly and frequently through all available communication networks. If a mission can be appropriately encapsulated in a slogan or catch phrase, it is more likely to be remembered. Slogans, however, can be overused and can produce a negative effect. They must be considered with caution.

If the leader communicates the mission, versus letting others "find it out" or leaving it up to chance to permeate the company, the mission will have greater impact than might otherwise be enjoyed. The leader should, without question, make communicating the mission the number-one priority in all talks and presentations to members of the group, either personally or via another media. The more a mission is personalized by the leader the better. Take the 1980 presidential election for example.

A few authoritative political analysts believe that President Reagan did not win the national election in 1980 because his mission was more acceptable than Carter's to the majority of American people; they feel he won because he did a superior job of articulating his mission. From the day he left the governorship of California to the day he won the election, Reagan accepted speaking engagements in every part of the United States. Not only did his mission (to return to a more conservative America) capture his audiences, it became more and more motivating to the future President himself.

Some observers suggest that the success of a mission depends more on articulation (90 percent) than on content (10 percent). They are quick to point out that making a profit is the true mission of any business enterprise. Yet this mission is never fully articulated. Workers are not reminded that if their firm does not win in the marketplace, their jobs are in jeopardy; that if the firm cannot make money, there will be no capital for growth, which in turn creates more opportunities. As a mission statement, "making a profit" is probably inspiring only to those who benefit directly—stockholders and employees who participate in profit-sharing plans. But put another way, the profit motive can inspire all: "Every day that we stay ahead of the competition, we move closer to profitability for everyone" or "When the company makes a profit, we all win." These are the kind of positive statements workers like to hear.

It is the responsibility of all leaders to lead the group in the direction that will provide the greatest benefit for all. But the meaning of both *benefit* and *direction* must be understood by the group. If not, team members may follow another course. And as it was pointed out in the great fable, *Alice in Wonderland*: "It doesn't make any difference which road you take if you don't know where you are going." It is only when leaders constantly communicate where they are headed, why they are going there, and what it will mean when they arrive that they are fulfilling their leadership potential.

Leaders who abdicate the opportunity to establish and articulate a mission are letting both themselves and their followers down. They are backing away from the heart of leadership.

MISSIONS AND POSITIVE FORCE

The Leadership Formula and the Leadership Strategic Model graphic illustrate that a winning mission becomes an extension of the positive force and power of influence communicated by the leader. Although some good missions are the result of group consensus (recommended), leaders must often create their own missions, without help. After all, leaders have the view from the top and thus the advantage of perspective.

In using their talents to come up with a mission, leaders must recognize that each group or organization—business, education, government, religious, community—should create its own special mission. To copy the mission of another group is to miss the point. And a mission should always have the personal stamp of its leader. It should grow out of and reflect his or her positive force.

Superior leaders find much of their motivation from the very missions they develop. Missions are, therefore, self-serving. They can, and often do, motivate the leader more than the followers. And that's not a bad endorsement.

SUMMARY

* A mission is more than a goal. It reflects the overriding purpose of the organization or institution. It should inspire both leaders and followers.
* A mission has three purposes: to motivate followers, to hold a group together, and to head the group in the right direction.
* Sometimes a primary organizational goal can be converted into a mission.
* Articulating a mission can be as important as the mission itself.
* Practical, short-term productivity goals can be effective when tied to an overriding mission.
* A mission is at the pinnacle of the leadership star and should be an extension of the power of influence created by the leader.

Case 15: Sub-Missions

Professor Robinson is a master teacher. His course on leadership and policy analysis is extremely popular. Maria, an office manager, age 26, is one of his assertive students. After a lecture on the importance of mission to the leadership concept, Maria volunteered this comment:

"I can understand why top leaders need to create a mission to motivate subordinates and to keep the organization alive and moving in the right direction, but I think it should stop there. Those of us at the bottom who run small departments should spend our time carrying out the big missions sent down to us. Creating one of our own is a joke."

Professor Robinson answered: "Does this mean that as an office manager you could not benefit from a tailor-made mission for just your employees? Isn't it possible that you could accept the company mission and at the same time create a smaller, but still effective, one of your own? What I'm leading up to is this. Sometimes a departmental mission will do more to create team spirit than a corporate mission handed down from above. You could try to be the most efficient department, most envied, or most friendly. If you succeeded, it would give the department an identity, and members would feel they belonged to a winner."

Maria replied: "Everyone in our outfit is goal-happy. I get so many goals handed down to me, I don't have time to develop any special mission. It would just be another responsibility. Besides, my employees are too sophisticated—they'd just laugh at the idea."

Professor Robinson continued: "I believe that creating a mission might be highly motivating to you, Maria. You might be more enthusiastic about a mission you created yourself than a big one that trickled down from above. I'm not sure that a mission at the bottom of an organization is not a good idea. It might make as much sense as one from the top. And it might contribute to productivity more than the company's mission."

Assume that you are a member of the class and Professor Robinson calls on you for your opinion. How would you reply? Would you support Maria or the professor? (The authors' opinions are given in the back of the book.)

Ramona Garcia, a hospital administrator, developed a mission statement for the 140-bed facility she supervises: "Better care—lower prices." Ms. Garcia tried out her mission statement on both internal and community groups. It was a great success. She then suggested to Louise Loring, her director of human resources, that she ask all hospital managers to develop a mission statement of their own. Ms. Garcia was careful to explain that departmental missions should follow the general mission in theme and certainly not conflict with it.

Case 16: Involvement

Ms. Loring is a believer in participatory management. She quickly called a conference of the sixteen managers representing various medical and nonmedical services. In presenting the idea she pointed out that establishing and maintaining a mission is a demonstration of good leadership. She also was able to get the group to agree on the following: (1) Missions must be expressed as short statements. (2) They must be accepted by the majority of departmental personnel. (3) They must be submitted within fifteen days. (4) All slogans will be posted in a public place so that everyone will know the mission of each department. (5) A winner will be selected, and those in the winning department will receive an extra day off with pay.

How would you evaluate this approach? Do you think it will be successful? What changes would you make? (See the back of the book for the authors' suggestions.)

Self-Test　　　　　　Mark the statements True (T) or False (F).

_____ 1. A goal and a mission are the same thing.

_____ 2. There is little relationship between a mission and a leader's power of influence.

_____ 3. Peter Drucker states that all organizations can benefit from a single, clear organizational mission.

_____ 4. Sometimes having too many goals makes it more difficult to have a single mission.

_____ 5. Visionary goal setters can get the job done even though a vision or mission may not be achieved.

_____ 6. Winning in itself cannot be a mission.

_____ 7. Sometimes it is much easier to create a mission than to articulate it.

_____ 8. Goals can never be converted into missions.

_____ 9. Reading is an excellent way to expand one's knowledge base for becoming more flexible, innovative, creative, and decisive.

_____10. A mission can be an adventure; a goal can be a chore.

Turn to the back of the book to check your answers.

TOTAL CORRECT _____

9 Create a Positive Force

Management works in the system; Leadership works on the system.*
Stephen R. Covey

*Covey, Stephen R., A. Roger Merrill, and Rebecca R. Merrill, First Things First. *New York: Simon & Schuster, 1994, p. 263.*

9 Create a Positive Force

SUCCESSFUL LEADERS GENERATE WAVES OF ACTIVITY

Drawing upon all power sources, especially personality power, a leader creates and maintains a positive force that pulls followers in a specified direction with enthusiasm and dedication. The strength of that positive force is, to a large degree, dependent upon one's attitude. A leader with an extraordinary, positive attitude can generate a strong power of influence—becoming an extremely powerful force that people want to follow.

Nothing is ever dull or routine in the presence of a true leader. Things are always jumping! The surroundings literally "feel" alive and dynamic. The positive force that radiates from the leader seems to be the very essence of his or her personality. And the positive force seen by others appears firmly grounded in the leader's physical, psychological, social, and spiritual well-being. Stephen Covey suggests that when our physical, mental, social, and spiritual needs overlap, "we find true inner balance, deep fulfillment, and joy."*

A positive attitude, then, is a direct outgrowth of our needs being fulfilled. Thus, it is no accident that a leader's positive force forms the nucleus of the star in our Leadership Strategic Model (Chapter 3).

> A positive attitude
> is central
> to a leader's positive force.

In creating an intensity of power, the leader must make maximum use of his or her communication system, see that followers receive proper rewards, make decisive decisions, and keep the mission in focus. Not an easy combination! Although all points in the star are equally important and interrelated, the energy that keeps them functioning at optimal level emanates from the center.

A POSITIVE ATTITUDE AS THE DRIVING FORCE

A leader's leadership power is fueled by a positive attitude. The more positive one's attitude is, the more it energizes and illuminates the star. Like any power system (generator, battery storing an electrical charge, etc.), the central force is what keeps the mechanism running.

---

*Covey, Stephen R., A. Roger Merrill, and Rebecca R. Merrill, First Things First. *New York: Simon & Schuster, 1994, p. 47.*

The positive force keeps a communication network alive. The positive force provides the vehicles to deliver rewards. The positive force creates good decisions. And drawing heavily from the three main power sources—role, personality, and knowledge—the positive force leads the organization to high productivity and success. Working together, the leader's positive force moves everything and everyone in the direction of a preestablished mission!

Most leaders put forth considerable effort in developing their power of influence. They rely on their strengths and use them to good advantage. And they also know they must turn their weaknesses into strengths. Keeping a positive attitude is absolutely critical to their success. Consider Cynthia's situation:

When Cynthia started her first season as a high school girls' soccer coach, she was very naive, nervous, and had little hope of success. Only a few young ladies turned out initially, and they were an undisciplined bunch. Her heart was in her stomach as she coached their first few practice sessions. It was not going to be easy to develop a real team.

Cynthia, however, was determined that things would improve. Because of her positive attitude, she soon built a pleasant relationship with each of her players. The players began to have fun at practice and started working together as a team. After winning a few games, the team seemed to work even harder on building skill, confidence, and poise. The day Cynthia told her fellow high school coaches that she intended to win the conference title, they laughed. But when the season was over, her team had the trophy to prove it.

Cynthia is no ordinary coach. She knows that most leaders have many enviable characteristics: most are intelligent, perceptive, personable, self-motivating, and courageous. She doesn't downplay these traits, but she

knows that there is one other critical trait that most people never think of when describing leadership.

It is the ability to create a positive force. And a positive force is based on a positive attitude.

In contrast to the other coaches, Cynthia had created, communicated, and maintained a consistent positive force. Her team, without knowing it, was caught up in something that made them reach beyond their everyday potential as competitors. It was Cynthia's positive force that had made the difference in their season.

A DYNAMIC SYNERGY

What, then, really is a positive force? In one sense, a positive force is nothing more than positive expectations. But, in another sense, it is a dynamic force that emanates from a leader and pulls the entire group into an inner circle of involvement and activity. Once it gets started, it seems to generate vigor and confidence. It stirs people up. It motivates. It removes obstacles. It leads to constructive action. It is, in effect, a form of energy. A positive force gets people on the right track and keeps them moving. It stems from the positive attitude of the leader, but it manifests itself in action.

Once a positive force gets under way, a group psychology takes over. Like a cyclone or tornado, it picks up momentum. Although it seems to feed on itself, the increased velocity comes from the dynamics (contributions) of the members of the group. A team results—a team or group of individuals that pull together toward a common goal. As the force increases in velocity, synergy is created. That is, there is a combined action. Often, the synergy is greater than the sum of each of the team's efforts. The positive force radiates beyond the team and it becomes extremely difficult to stand on the sidelines and not be drawn into the activity.

When there is an absence of positive, forceful leadership, lethargy takes over. The sensation of motion disappears. Lassitude prevails. The organization or group becomes sluggish and fat. In reference to the Leadership Formula (depicted by the Leadership Strategic Model), the tips of the star begin to sag, the star begins to shrink, and the luster disappears. When a slump occurs, followers are left uninspired and, ultimately, disenchanted.

AVOIDING A NEGATIVE FORCE

When leadership does not generate a consistent positive force, those required to exist inside organizational frameworks usually relax. They mark time. And they take the course of least resistance.

Nothing separates a manager from a leader more than being able to create and maintain a positive force. Managers can often survive through controls, efficiency, and "good management" of an operation. A leader must be sufficiently dynamic to create a force that will carry the organization to new heights. It is the leader who must be the cheerleader—an upbeat person with a positive attitude!

How is a positive force created? Leaders create the force in their individual ways. They glamorize their role positions, making them the center of action. They use their knowledge to get followers to use their research and inquiry skills to be more creative and innovative. They turn their personality power loose, sending rays of energy in all directions. They show personal vigor. They demonstrate a bearing that communicates strength. They create the feeling that something good is about to happen.

CREATING A POSITIVE FORCE

CHARGE

Like a pebble dropped into a quiet pool, the power of your positive attitude starts the force, but it is your special characteristics that push it into wider and wider circles. Each leader must develop his or her own centrifugal-power configuration, employing all positive personality characteristics and elements to keep the force alive.

> A leader's positive force
> always starts
> with a positive attitude.

Remaining positive under trying conditions is not an easy task. Yet, if you wish to be a successful leader, you have no choice. You must remain positive because your positive attitude is the source of the power. Your positive attitude communicates to those you lead that they are headed in the right direction, that there are exciting goals within reach, that something better lies over the horizon. A positive attitude in a leader builds positive expectations in the minds of the group, whereas a negative attitude destroys them. When a leader turns negative, the positive force dissipates as quickly as the air in a punctured balloon.

LEADERS ARE ALWAYS ON CENTER STAGE

Because leaders transmit much of their positive force through their presence or personality, they must always be "up" so that their followers will never feel "down."

"I can let my negative feelings show to my secretary and immediate staff, but never to my employees."

"You can never let down in front of the troops."

"When I'm not up, neither is the team."

"Leadership and being positive are inseparable."

Being constantly on center stage can make or break a leader, especially in the world of politics, where the pressure is intense and the stage is always in the public eye. But center stage visibility likewise is important for many other people—coaches, corporate leaders, youth workers, clergy, and others in leadership roles. Whatever your leadership position may be, now or in the future, the responsibility of being in the limelight will have more meaning after your complete the "Press Conference" exercise that follows.

PRESS CONFERENCE

To establish yourself as a positive force, you must communicate the impression that you are in charge whenever you are in the presence of others. To help you learn this skill, assume you are the subject of a televised press conference. All eyes are on you as you walk into the studio.

List in order of priority the impressions you would like to project to your audience, placing (in the left column) a "1" next to the characteristic you feel most important, a "2" for second important, etc. In the right-hand column, rank in order of priority the characteristics you need to work on the most to improve your "center stage" image.

Priority		*Work Needed*
_____	positive attitude	_____
_____	imperturbability	_____
_____	vigor	_____
_____	positive bearing	_____
_____	friendliness	_____
_____	excellent speaking ability	_____
_____	good grammar and diction	_____
_____	good listening skills	_____
_____	perceptiveness	_____
_____	knowledge	_____
_____	sincerity and honesty	_____
_____	sense of humor	_____
_____	good grooming	_____
_____	decisiveness	_____

Now compare the numbers you assigned to each item. If you entered a low number (indicating the item is a high priority) on both sides of a factor, any improvement you make in that area will pay double dividends in creating a stronger in-charge impression.

PERSONALITY AND VOICE POWER

Personality power plays a leading role in the development of a positive force. One of the best ways to "see" personality power is in body language. A person's eye contact, posture and stance, gesturing, and voice are but a few ways one can quickly assess a leader's personality power. You could probably name several individuals who, because of their body language, portray a take-charge image. The force of take-charge people frequently can be felt immediately—as you enter their presence, their offices, or even large meetings where they may be speaking. With some leaders, the power is so forceful it is almost like you have walked into a magnetic field.

While body language, grooming, and diction communicate personal power, it is frequently the leader's voice that communicates the most power. That is, a leader can be very impressive if his or her tone and speaking manner communicates a positive force. Many leaders deliberately use their voices to impress others with their leadership strength. Voice can be a very strong personality power. Leaders who develop their voice power have mastered a very dynamic leadership characteristic.

PERSONAL ACTIVITY CONTRIBUTES TO A POSITIVE FORCE

Successful leaders are always on the move. They transfer their positive attitudes into physical action. They create a flurry of activity that has a domino effect. Their momentum sets the tempo for others to follow.

Leaders operate in the sea of activity they themselves create and then watch it flow throughout their organization. Here is the way one executive secretary describes her boss, a recognized leader:

> The only time you will find things peaceful around here is when she is on a trip. She thrives on activity, and it's catching. I sometimes feel I'm in the center of a hurricane. Everyone here at the home office knows immediately when she is back from a trip. In fact, we feel the storm coming ahead of time.

There are two kinds of delegating. One form is designed to get work done—to meet production schedules, publicity deadlines, and similar timelines. In the other form, motivational delegating, leaders assign projects, expect research to be done, ask for reports, and seek advice. Successful leaders are good delegators. They constantly keep people involved by giving them something new to do, frequently for the purpose of keeping them from getting bored.

Motivational delegating helps people reach their potential. Not that the tasks delegated do not need to be accomplished— most of them do. The idea of a motivational leader is to delegate enough that they keep people moving, creating, and releasing their talent and energy.

Motivational delegating usually enhances the positive force that is already alive. It keeps life in the group or organization. Leaders seem to sense that motivational delegating is an extension of their personal force. Here are several leaders' statements about motivational delegation:

> I motivate my people almost 100 percent through delegation. I cook up ideas that can't help but have a positive thrust for our organization—and then I turn them over to others. I never want anyone on my staff ever to catch up to the point of relaxing or being bored. They just wouldn't be happy.

> It's my responsibility as a leader to keep everyone moving, living at their capacity, contributing. I hate boredom myself, and it really galls me to see people idle. So if they don't have enough to do, I create it—for their good and the good of our firm.

> Inactivity always leads to trouble. I don't want my employees to live in a stressful climate, but I want them busy and involved in meaningful and productive endeavors.

It is obvious that executives cannot sit back and wait for their employees to energize themselves. Coaches cannot merely wait for their teams to catch fire. Clergy cannot expect their congregations to provide their own spiritual guidance. And community leaders cannot expect volunteers to motivate themselves. Leaders must step in and make things happen. Motivational delegating is the prime tool in their leadership kits to get people to utilize their expertise, energy, creativity, and talent.

Once created, how can the positive force be kept alive? Once there is movement, how can it be maintained? The answer is *communication*.

Without good communication, a positive force cannot get started, let alone thrive. The leader must set and maintain an effective organizational communication network. Without it, the positive force will die in the leader's office.

POSITIVE-FORCE CONTRACT
(Become a More Positive Force by Making a Contract with Yourself)

It is possible to become a more positive force in any leadership role—including as a parent or a community volunteer. In this exercise, you make a contract with yourself to demonstrate you can be a more positive force in the future. To be a more positive force means you will need to increase your enthusiasm and communicate a more positive posture and attitude. The recommended procedure is as follows:

Step 1. Find a suitable observer—someone who sees you in operation on a daily basis: your boss, a colleague, a mentor, a friend, or family member. Make sure it is a person you respect, who is familiar with your behavior patterns.

Step 2. Make an appointment with the person and explain that you have made a contract with yourself to extend your positive influence into wider circles. You are sincere in your desire to improve your leadership style. The reason for a structured meeting is to make certain the contract is not interpreted as a temporary or offhand decision.

Step 3. At the meeting, ask the individual if he or she will observe the way you behave during a thirty-day period. Ask him or her to tell you at the end of this period if he or she can sense any behavior modifications that indicate you are acting in a more positive manner. Also, ask the observer to keep mental or written notes during the period, but not talk to you about the experiment or tell anyone else about it.

Step 5. At the end of the thirty-day period, set up a second meeting to discuss the observations. Were behavior changes noticeable? Did others, not involved in the experiment, notice? Were all changes an improvement? What can be done to keep your positive force alive in the future?

Step 6. Evaluate the observer's comments and make a long-term contract with yourself for continued improvement.

A communication network keeps a leader in touch with the people he or she leads. It can include every kind of medium—from a personal note to a formal company newsletter, from a telephone call to a nationally televised public affairs program. A network is a media system that allows members of a group to be in on the action and leaders to keep in touch with the feelings of the group when personal contact is impossible.

A good communication network can keep everyone in tune with

organizational goals. Members of the group know where they are, why they are doing what they are doing, and what may happen down the road. They feel they belong.

Every organization, large or small, has its formal communication system. The following case illustrates how extensive and dynamic such a system can be.

> Peter Gomez is the newly hired president of a software distribution company. The company used a professional headhunter to find its new leader because the poor performance of its previous president convinced the board the firm needed proven talent. A new, fresh, positive force might put some life back into the company.
>
> When Mr. Gomez arrived, his first priority was to analyze the communication network. Total revamping was evident. Within thirty days, Mr. Gomez (1) replaced the communication officer; (2) set up a series of strategic planning meetings; (3) wrote the lead article for the next issue of the company's newsletter; (4) purchased video equipment for the training department and prepared six tapes to be shown to all employees; (5) scheduled a tour every week to inspect all eleven departments in the organization; (6) initiated a weekly bulletin outlining key developments of the previous week, to be distributed to all employees each Monday morning; (7) set aside every Friday afternoon from 3 to 5 for informal chats with employees; (8) asked his new communication officer to restyle the company newsletter; and (9) increased the communication budget.
>
> Although Mr. Gomez knew that he would not be able to maintain such a flurry of activity over a sustained period, he decided it was necessary to launch a positive force that would eventually turn the organization around. Without a new, revised communication network and considerable company reengineering, he felt he could not accomplish his goals, let alone a more lofty mission that both he and the board hoped would get the company back on track.

While Mr. Gomez's actions may have seemed excessive to you, he put into practice a basic leadership principle: create a positive force, motivate others to follow, and put a plan of decisive action into motion as quickly as possible. He used his positive force to show others he was in charge—and he wasn't afraid to personally take on a considerable share of the work to get it accomplished!

One way to perceive both the importance and difficulty of creating a positive force is to measure your own reaction to your manager or leader. To assess your reactions of the leader you are following, ask yourself these questions:

	Yes	No
1. Am I, as a subordinate or observer, caught up in the positive force created by the leader?	☐	☐
2. Can I sense the presence of the leader's positive force?	☐	☐
3. Has the leader created a dynamic, positive group acceptance of his or her leadership?	☐	☐
4. Are members of the group or team totally motivated to follow the leader?	☐	☐
5. Is the leader aware that he or she is constantly on stage?	☐	☐
6. Does the leader suppress negative and apathetic feelings?	☐	☐
7. Do I, guided by the leader, feel I am going somewhere?	☐	☐
8. Is the organization moving in a positive direction?	☐	☐
9. Does the leader generate an upbeat feeling among employees and managers alike?	☐	☐
10. Would I be willing to follow the leader in the face of strong opposition from others?	☐	☐
11. Does the leader make it easy for me to stay positive?	☐	☐
12. Does the leader have characteristics that I could benefit from emulating?	☐	☐

Tough questions? Yes! Yet they get to the essence of what true leadership is. If the majority of your answers to the questions (especially the last question) were "yes," you probably should continue to observe and assess the leader's qualities to help you with your own leadership development. However, if several of your answers were "no," you should find another person to serve as your role model.

Denis Waitley,* in his book, *Empires of the Mind: Lessons to Lead and Succeed in the Knowledge-Based World* says, "You can control who you choose as role models, and who you'll seek out for mentoring counseling and inspiration." His advise is sound. By observing and studying a

---

New York: William Morrow & Co., Inc., 1995, p. 32.

good role model, you can improve your own leadership skills—toward becoming a positive force.

Whatever leadership role you occupy or will assume in the future, you must, if you wish to be successful over the long term, accept the challenge of becoming a positive force. How powerful a force must you create, and how will you know it is adequate? Just turn around. If your followers are following, you're on the right track! And keep in mind that a positive force, driven by a positive attitude (along with other elements of the Leadership Formula), is the essence of leadership.

ACCEPT THE CHALLENGE

SUMMARY

* You cannot exist as a leader without developing a positive force that will inspire those who follow you.
* A positive force generates constructive action.
* Synergy relates to combined action; thus, when a positive force gets started, its effect can be widespread.
* A positive force stems from a positive attitude, which is at the heart of your personality power.
* Leaders need to show great energy.
* As a leader, you are always on center stage.
* Leaders use motivational delegating to capitalize on the talents, energy, and creativity of people.
* A good communication system permits the leader of a large organization to communicate his or her positive force to all members of the group, no matter how far away they may be.

Case 17: Charisma

Justine and Rebecca have been good friends since college days, when both prepared for careers in youth work. Justine is currently director of a YMCA in northern California. Rebecca is a Girl Scout executive for a large council in southern California. Both are attending a leadership seminar sponsored by a nationally known foundation. They are sitting around the dinner table discussing the importance of creating and maintaining a positive force. Justine comments:

"My observation tells me that charisma is the primary source of a positive force. This is especially true in youth activities because kids are so impressionable. If kids are to respond, there has to be a touch of magic in the leader's personality—something that makes the leader a role model. Without this, it's impossible for leaders to establish themselves as a moving force."

"You say that," replies Rebecca, "because you are long on charisma and you rely on it. What about plain Janes like me? Can we never be leaders just because we are not blessed with charisma? I believe we can lead if we develop good, positive attitudes. That is what young people want in a leader. Someone who looks at the good side and transmits confidence. Attitude is the answer, not charisma."

Do you support Justine or Rebecca? Why? Could you build a case that a positive attitude is a charismatic characteristic? (The authors' opinions are given in the back of the book.)

Fred Fisher, executive vice-president of a large utility, and Yali Grey, public relations officer for the same firm, are having lunch in the executive dining room.

"I agree with the positive force idea," states Fred, "and we are fortunate to have J.B. as our president. He really stays positive, moves around, and somehow provides us with the vision and force we need to keep growing. He is a remarkable leader and certainly makes my job easier."

"In a way that is true," replied Yali, "but the positive force he represents still needs to be communicated to our 9,000 employees, our stockholders, and customers. He cannot do this alone. In fact, it is about 10 percent effort on his part and 90 percent effort on our part. I agree he has a good image for us to transmit, but we still have to transmit it. J.B. still needs to be sold in every publication, on television, and in all media. You might say he creates a positive force, but we communicate it."

"You may be overstating your own importance. I believe the lowest employee we have would feel the positive force J.B. creates without any formal communication. A positive force is personality based, and it transmits itself more through the grapevine and personal contact than through the media. One employee catches it and passes it on to another. You're saying, in effect, that you manufacture the positive force that keeps this company moving."

"No, I'm saying that without a well-organized formal communication system, any positive force created by the top leader would eventually die on the vine. J.B. couldn't get his positive force beyond you and his personal staff without us. We enhance, maintain, and protect his image. We keep the force going."

"I'm not saying we should eliminate the PR department," said Fred, "but you totally underestimate how much J.B. does on his own."

Does Ms. Grey overstate her case? Does Mr. Fisher underestimate the importance of formal communication? Take a position on the problem and defend it. (The authors' suggestions are given in the back of the book.)

Self-Test

Mark each statement True (T) or False (F).

_____ 1. A positive force emanates from a leader and pulls followers into an inner circle of involvement.

_____ 2. Without a positive force created by leaders, members of a group will usually take the course of least resistance.

_____ 3. Only leaders have the capacity to create a force that people will follow.

_____ 4. A positive attitude is the primary source of a positive force.

_____ 5. It advisable for leaders to use their role and knowledge power to create a positive force, but not their personality power.

_____ 6. Synergy can be optimized as a result of a strong positive force.

_____ 7. The stronger the positive force, the higher productivity is apt to be.

_____ 8. The fact that "Positive Force" is at the center of the Leadership Strategic Model star means that it is central to successful leadership.

_____ 9. Leaders, whether they know it or not, are always on center stage.

_____ 10. A positive force transmits itself throughout an organization; thus, a communication network is not needed.

Turn to the back of the book to check your answers.

TOTAL CORRECT _____

10 Maximize Your Leadership Style

A critic is a man who knows the way, but can't drive the car.

Kenneth Tynan

⟨10⟩ Maximize Your Leadership Style

DO IT YOUR WAY

Henry and his partner, Jake, are having their regular morning meeting to discuss operational problems in their chain of restaurants. Today the discussion centers on the problem of training managers.

"Ten years ago," Henry remarks, "we had the time and money to conduct in-house seminars and give our new managers a lot of personal help. Today, with tighter budgets, all we can do is establish the best possible working environment, provide the tools, and hope they will train themselves."

Jake agrees. "If those in our organization who want to be leaders are not self-motivated, there is little we can do to help them."

Henry and Jake have a point.

You could be a national political leader, a corporate executive, a first-line supervisor, a religious leader, a community leader, etc. You could also be on the sidelines, a student preparing to be a leader. Whatever your position, if you want to become a better leader and are not self-motivated, you are in trouble. That is the bad news.

The good news is that if you really want to put more leadership into your style, you can do so. The Leadership Formula (Leadership Strategic Model) provides the guidelines, but you must realize it is a do-it-yourself project.

How you go about weaving the Leadership Formula into your style will depend upon your experience and the role you occupy. It will also depend upon your understanding of your own leadership style and those of others.

BASIC APPROACHES TO ACTION: PART OF YOUR LEADERSHIP STYLE

Your leadership style is dependent upon many interrelated factors—making decisive decisions, being an effective communicator, having a positive attitude, etc.—the components of the Leadership Formula. In addition, there are three basic approaches that describe your actions for everything you do, including how you lead.

What approach guides your actions? Do you command or "direct" actions—yours as well as others? Do you take a "permissive" approach to your everyday life; that is, do you just let things happen? Do your actions suggest you prefer to play a "support" role and help others meet their goals? Or, depending on the situation, do your actions encompass more than one approach? Your actions (as well as inaction) influence how you interact with your family, friends, superiors, fellow workers, and subordinates (including the followers you have empowered).

It follows that if you can identify the basic approach that describes your own actions as well as understand why other people "do as they do," you will add yet another insight toward maximizing your leadership style. Here are the three approaches that describe a person's actions.

1. Direct Approach. In the direct approach, a person takes a "no-nonsense" approach to almost everything he or she does. As a leader whose style follows a direct approach, the leader tells others what is expected of them. There is a definite plan of action outlined. The goals are set and are clear. There are specific and frequently detailed timelines for completion (and, as appropriate, due dates for progress reports). There are objectives which prioritize the tasks to be completed and specific actions to be taken.

In the direct approach the leader is basically a one-way communicator. That is, she or he covers the "who, what, when, why, where, how" by telling employees what to do, how to do it, etc. Frequently, the leader may show employees how he or she wants the job done. The leader also communicates what the results should be and tells employees how and on what factors their performance will be evaluated.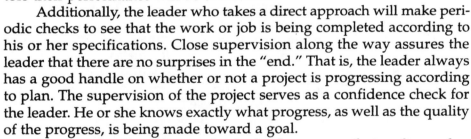

Additionally, the leader who takes a direct approach will make periodic checks to see that the work or job is being completed according to his or her specifications. Close supervision along the way assures the leader that there are no surprises in the "end." That is, the leader always has a good handle on whether or not a project is progressing according to plan. The supervision of the project serves as a confidence check for the leader. He or she knows exactly what progress, as well as the quality of the progress, is being made toward a goal.

Thus, in the direct approach, the leader assures that each member of the team knows exactly what he or she needs to do, when and how it is to be done, where quality checks will be applied, and how performance and productivity will be measured. The roles are very clear.

2. Permissive Approach. Many people demonstrate a permissive approach in their daily lives as well as in tackling work tasks. The individuals following this style usually are those who operate in a very free environment. That is, a person espousing the permissive approach may be very laid back and just lets things happen.

On the other hand, there are also many gregarious, happy, fun-loving people that practice a permissive approach. These positive, outgoing people enjoy life; and their personalities overshadow the fact that they may be jumping from one activity to another without much follow-through. Their personality is so positive, they charm everyone around them. If they are sincere, well meaning, and motivating to others, they

often get others to take up the slack and pull more than their share of the load—frequently without even realizing it!

The permissive approach is characterized by an individual who "sees a field of flowers" (no weeds) and who lets the moment dictate his or her actions. The permissive leader permits followers to direct their own actions. Sometimes sub-leaders emerge. When sub-leaders take charge, the leader can be effective because the permissive approach has empowered followers (sub-leaders) to get the job done.

With (but usually without) a sub-leader, the permissive approach may be attractive to employees—especially at the outset of a project, when one joins a new team, or at the time of initial employment for an organization. Over time, however, employees usually want more structure.

A permissive approach to leadership depends on employee self-motivation. Usually a "do-as-you-wish" premise to work accomplishment neither reaps desirable results nor provides employees with long-term motivation. If the company does not employ other motivating factors (such as a strong mission that is exciting to employees or a reward system for productivity), employees lose interest in their work. They work for a paycheck; and they may not enjoy the benefits of job satisfaction. Their productivity is not maximized, and they probably do not see any benefit of being a contributing team member.

The permissive approach to leadership, in its purest sense, can be described as a nonleadership approach. And, for the most part, leaders who take the permissive approach will not remain in leadership positions very long. Followers want a leader who exercises "leadership"—a leader who is a visionary, who can make decisive decisions, and who can effectively develop and communicate a vital mission. They want a leader who, with a positive force and power of influence, will empower them and implement a mutual reward system. They want a leader who makes a difference—someone who is more than a cheerleader. The permissive approach does none of these things.

3. Support Approach. A leader who capitalizes on a support approach truly is a coach. The coach knows when to listen and is a good listener. Employees know they can go to the leader with any type of problem; they know they will get support and encouragement from their "coach." Interaction through two-way communication is a key factor for the leader who uses the support approach. Thus, the leader or coach becomes a good facilitator.

Facilitation differs from the direct approach in that the leader does not tell the workers exactly what to do, but solicits suggestions and input—frequently in team meetings—to get the job done. Followers have direct input into decision making. They benefit from the rewards of being self-directed with a supportive leader who praises them for a job well done. The leader offers encouragement all along the way, especially when workers seem to need that little boost.

The leader does not do progress checks in a traditional manner. He or she is able to stay "on top" of progress toward a goal by involving workers in discussions and team meetings. The time spent in team meetings is productive because everyone is a stakeholder and shares in the process. The leader/facilitator frequently is the one whose team comes up with the best suggestion to build a better mouse trap—improving both processes and productivity. They maximize productivity as a team.

With the support approach, the leader encourages and promotes team involvement that permeates beyond the team. Synergy is maximized. Quality, high standards, and motivation are all part of the standard mode of operation. Similarly, evaluation of performance is a built-in element—it goes with the territory of good leadership and empowered followers.

A BLEND OF THE APPROACHES

While distinct differences have been pointed out between the direct, permissive, and support approaches, most people's actions do not always "fit" into one distinct category. Most have a blend of the approaches, with one approach dominating their actions and their leadership styles.

Knowing your style—the basic or primary approach that you follow—should be important to you for two reasons: (1) You understand yourself better when you know what approach governs your actions toward accomplishing goals; (2) You have a better appreciation of others who have styles that differ from yours. As you become cognizant of others' needs and how they approach things, you can learn to adapt your approach to promote better communication toward building strong relationships.

Keep in mind that the direct approach and the support approach can be equally effective. Also, if you become astutely aware of the pitfalls of the permissive approach, it, too, may be used with caution. Once you have identified the approach which drives your leadership style, you will be able to see more clearly the approaches taken by other people.

Understanding your own style is the first step toward adapting (and modifying as needed) your approach to day-to-day situations. To be an effective leader, your approach should be clear to followers. There also must be a flexible element in your style so you can maximize your approach. It is that "fine-tuned balance" that is critical to a situation. As each situation dictates, you begin to practice situational leadership. Situational leadership is learned with practice by putting all the leadership essentials to work.

So, what is your dominant approach that drives your leadership style? Can you easily identify the approach which describes the actions of a leader you admire or a leader you may follow as a role model? As you gain understanding of the approaches that are at the very underpinnings of your leadership style, you will be able to see why certain actions (and reactions) result. It is this level of understanding that is extremely important to maximize your leadership effectiveness.

THE LEADERSHIP STAR MODEL

Leadership effectiveness is not built in a day, a week, or a month—it takes effort and practice over time. Leadership ability develops as one internalizes and practices each of the elements represented in the Leadership Formula as illustrated in the Leadership Strategic Model (star). If you accept the Model which communicates the very essence of leadership, it becomes a reference point for personal and professional growth and development.

One way to use the Leadership Formula is to adopt it as your own and use it as a guide for growing into management and leadership roles. That is, use it to balance management with leadership skills, for self-evaluation when progress is slow, and to keep dreams and aspirations alive. And, above all, use it to boost your positive attitude. The star can and should become your own Model for long-term career development.

PINPOINTING STRENGTHS AND WEAKNESSES

For those who already occupy management or leadership roles, the Leadership Strategic Model star illustration can indicate areas of weakness where immediate improvement would pay large dividends. Although it is possible to show improvement in all areas shown in the Model, experience indicates that many leaders have neglected (without knowing it) one or two of the elements.

The following exercise, My Leadership Development Priorities, can be used to identify your leadership strengths and weaknesses. The authors challenge you to complete the exercise and to let the results help guide you toward greater leadership effectiveness.

MY LEADERSHIP DEVELOPMENT PRIORITIES

Once people become acquainted with the fundamentals in the Leadership Formula (the star illustration of the Leadership Strategic Model), they sense the point of their greatest weakness(es). Complete the following activity by placing a "1" in the appropriate box of the star representing the top priority area where improvement will do most for your leadership image. Then place numbers 2, 3, 4, 5, and 6 in the remaining squares in the order you perceive self-improvement is needed. Prioritizing your areas of greatest need should establish the order in which you intend to take action toward maximizing your leadership style.

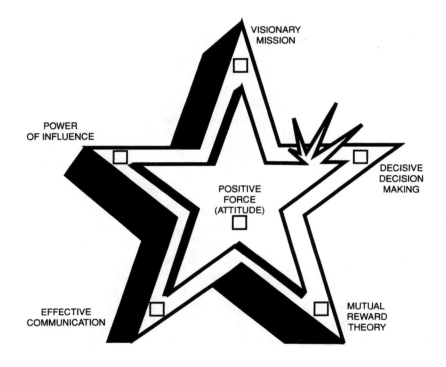

As you assess the areas which need your greatest effort, review the chapters of the book relating to those elements. Then read more widely on your selected area(s) of development. Make a weekly goal (and write it down to review it often) to work on a specific task toward improving your skills of your identified element(s). Make your self-improvement exercise a part of your on-going daily activities to maximize your leadership style every day!

You are well aware that self-improvement activities are extremely important to your well-being. Everyone needs to get an adrenaline boost from time to time, especially because our society seems to thrive on negatives—maybe it's because we haven't learned to sensationalize positive actions! Ask yourself three questions: Do I like to be around positive people? Can I be a more upbeat and vibrant person? Can I (as well as others) benefit from improving my leadership skills?

As a reader of this book, the authors assume your answers are "yes." Now, what are your immediate plans for further action toward self-improvement? Here are the actions taken by John, Anne, and Xavier.

When, as the result of a seminar, John took a look at the Leadership Formula, he became aware that he had lost his punch as a positive force. His attitude was not as positive at it should be; and, as a result, his leadership had become less effective in the other five areas. John decided to take action and adopt the Leadership Formula as his own. He reactivated himself as a dynamic force and was, once again, on the move.

Anne attended the same seminar. She, too, became aware that she had not provided her followers with a mission to which they could tie their immediate goals. Thus, after the seminar, she did some serious rethinking about the direction her organization was taking. At her next staff meeting, Anne articulated a new mission that not only motivated her group but gave her more enthusiasm.

It took a management course and the Leadership Formula to convince Xavier that he had not developed or adequately used his power of influence. Because he took immediate action, similar to John and Anne, Xavier returned to his leadership role with more confidence and renewed determination to become a leader/manager instead of simply a manager.

Each person, of course, has his or her own interpretation of the Leadership Formula (illustrated by the star of the Leadership Strategic Model). And everyone decides how and when they may or may not weave all or part of it into their behavioral pattern. Experience shows that most leaders who are exposed to the Formula for the first time discover at least one weakness that they decide to strengthen.

If for no other reason, the Leadership Formula should provide a guide for your leadership awareness. If you wish to adopt the Formula as your own, it is also a powerful "tool" for assessing your leadership strengths and weaknesses. The Formula becomes particularly useful when you apply it along with a good understanding of your basic style (direct, permissive, or support approach). The self-improvement process begins with your desire to maximize your leadership. The next step is to mobilize your desire.

There are also other advantages associated with the use of the Leadership Strategic Model (Leadership Formula). The Model, as the essence of leadership, can be used to evaluate the leadership effectiveness of others. Comparing one leader's strengths and weaknesses with another is especially valuable. (If you have difficulty in identifying leaders, start with one or two political leaders. The media, no doubt, will have a considerable influence on how each one compares with the other.)

To help you identify the factors or items for rating leaders, refer to the Leadership Effectiveness Scale that follows. You can use the exercise to evaluate yourself as well as for assessing the leadership effectiveness of others. The scale is of special value when you rate yourself first. Then ask another person to assess your skills using the scale and make a comparison of the results. Next, plan a course of action that you can take to improve your leadership skills. The scale reflects the essence of leadership as communicated in the Leadership Formula.

RATING OTHERS AS WELL AS YOURSELF

LEADERSHIP EFFECTIVENESS SCALE

INSTRUCTIONS

Here are thirty-six (36) practices commonly demonstrated by acknowledged leaders. Read each statement carefully. Decide the extent to which you practice each characteristic by circling the appropriate number to the right of each practice.

(My Name)	Strongly Agree	Somewhat Agree	Somewhat Disagree	Strongly Disagree
1. Keeps followers fully informed.	4	3	2	1
2. Expresses thoughts clearly and forcefully.	4	3	2	1
3. Speaks well from a platform.	4	3	2	1
4. Is a good listener.	4	3	2	1
5. Attracts others to want to hear what he/she has to say.	4	3	2	1
6. Communicates a sense of "being in charge."	4	3	2	1
7. Develops employees into followers.	4	3	2	1
8. Demonstrates compassion for others.	4	3	2	1
9. Provides rewards that are important to followers.	4	3	2	1
10. Strives to win by allowing followers to win also.	4	3	2	1
11. Attracts others to want to join his/her group.	4	3	2	1
12. Has the full backing of all those who work under him/her.	4	3	2	1

	Strongly Agree	Somewhat Agree	Somewhat Disagree	Strongly Disagree
13. Provides enough structure to create a cohesive feeling among her/his subordinates.	4	3	2	1
14. Establishes an authority line that is clear, consistent, and appropriate for the situation.	4	3	2	1
15. Utilizes role, personality, and knowledge power in a balanced, effective manner.	4	3	2	1
16. Gets tough when necessary.	4	3	2	1
17. Is respected by subordinates when authority is used.	4	3	2	1
18. Uses the power that he/she has with firmness but also with sensitivity.	4	3	2	1
19. Consults with others before making important decisions.	4	3	2	1
20. Has a strong track record for making solid decisions.	4	3	2	1
21. Follows a logical pattern in making decisions.	4	3	2	1
22. Stages and communicates decisions with pride and decisiveness.	4	3	2	1
23. Is able to admit mistakes when he/she makes them.	4	3	2	1
24. Faces up to and makes hard decisions.	4	3	2	1
25. Always maintains an upbeat, positive attitude.	4	3	2	1
26. Articulates an inspiring mission to all employees/followers.	4	3	2	1
27. Generates a feeling of pride and higher productivity in followers.	4	3	2	1
28. Ties short-term work goals to inspirational missions.	4	3	2	1
29. Makes work more enjoyable.	4	3	2	1
30. Shares both large and small victories with followers.	4	3	2	1
31. Gets others caught up in his/her positive force.	4	3	2	1
32. Creates an active tempo that others want to emulate.	4	3	2	1
33. Reflects a positive attitude during difficult or tough times.	4	3	2	1
34. Is highly energetic and refuses to be "desk bound."	4	3	2	1

	Strongly Agree	Somewhat Agree	Somewhat Disagree	Strongly Disagree
35. Inspires others to be all they can be.	4	3	2	1
36. If she/he resigned, others would want to follow.	4	3	2	1

Turn to page 172 for scoring instructions. (A duplicate form also is provided in the back of the book for you to have another person rate you on each of the characteristics.)

Should none of the leadership development suggestions described above fall within your comfort zone, you may decide to use the Leadership Formula in your own way. You may, of course, decide that you prefer to remain a manager or a follower. Whatever your decision is, what you have learned about leadership will help you assess the effectiveness of those who have decided to take the risk that goes along with leadership. Either way, you come out ahead.

TAKING THE NEXT STEP: FORGE AHEAD

Assuming you decide to accept the challenge to maximize your leadership and start enhancing your leadership capabilities, you will want to tread lightly and consider the following three suggestions.

A POST SCRIPT

1. Protect Your Flanks. After a well-known entertainer purchased an expensive fur coat at an exclusive boutique in New York, she asked to use the telephone to call her insurance agent to make arrangements to have the fur insured immediately. As she hung up the telephone, she remarked to the salesperson, "I need the fur for my image, but I've got to recognize it might be ripped off at any moment."

Because leaders must be aware they are always on center stage, they have something of the same problem as the entertainer who purchased the fur coat. They must create and maintain an image, but they must accept the fact that some members of the group might, at any time, turn against them. They cannot, unfortunately, purchase insurance for protection, but they must constantly be aware that a disenchanted subordinate might try to undermine them.

Divisiveness and jealousy on the part of those who may resent you as a leader or anyone in a leadership position goes with the leadership territory. There will always be those who resent you because they weren't able to climb the leadership ladder. Also, beware that you may not get the same support as many said they would give you when you become their leader.

As you enter your new (or expand your present) role as a leader, your position in itself changes your relationships with everyone in the organization. By capitalizing on your personality power (as well as your knowledge power), your leadership role should be one that is an exciting challenge. If you maximize (and continue to develop) each of the areas in the Leadership Strategic Model, you will enjoy good relationships and become a strong leader.

Strong leadership requires that emphasis be placed on establishing an effective and consistent two-way communication network. In addition to transmitting the positive force created by the leader, your network must uncover potentially dangerous counter forces so that some form of corrective action can be taken before things get out of hand. Here's an example of the importance of a good communication network.

> Mary Mullins, mayor of a community of over 50,000 residents, was determined to cut down on crime. To this end, she beefed up the resources of the police department. Her efforts paid off handsomely; but other city employees, especially those in the fire department, started to feel neglected and even hostile.
>
> It was fortunate for Ms. Mullins that she received a signal through her communication system that all was not well. She immediately set up a meetings with the fire chief and other key staff, started to visit outlying fire stations, and even had the local newspaper run a series of feature articles on the work of the mayor's office starting with the fire department. Her communication network came to her rescue before things got out of hand.

The moment you make the transition to a leadership position, you become a target. You lose the anonymity you enjoyed as a member of the group. You become a topic of conversation in all types of social settings—from coffee klatches, lunch groups, and cocktail parties to sports events, locker rooms, and bars.

As a member of a group, you were comfortable. You had more security, fewer responsibilities, and time to relax and enjoy your colleagues. As a leader, you must try to provide the rewards the members of the group desire, but you have less security yourself. You also have less time and opportunity for casual conversations. Everything suddenly becomes more formal. You find yourself dependent upon your communication system to keep an ear to the ground.

You probably can see why it is important for top political leaders to have press agents and public relations specialists. These media specialists help politicians create and monitor the positive force that keeps them in office. Even with the assistance they receive, they frequently get into trouble.

If you are a first-line supervisor, a middle manager, a coach, or a volunteer leader, you may not have a staff surrounding you to provide the communication assistance and protection you desire or need. You may have to do it yourself, quickly discovering that it is far easier to create positive momentum than to keep it going.

2. Work within Your Comfort Zone. In becoming a leader, it is important to *do it your way.* That is, stay within the framework of your own personality and your own style. Your comfort zone should not be interpreted, however, as not moving into uncharted waters. Quite the contrary. You should always challenge yourself to higher levels. But while you are stepping out into new and somewhat strange territory, do it within the established framework that works for you.

With each challenge that you meet within your ability levels, you will gradually expand your comfort zone. It gets bigger and bigger with effort and practice. Thus, you can become an effective communicator, an outstanding decision maker, and a positive force without turning yourself upside down. The idea is to start where you are and strengthen yourself in each of the areas represented by the Leadership Formula.

3. Maintain Your Management Competence. Whatever your degree of management competence, you are encouraged to build your leadership competence on your management skills. That is, you must stay current with management developments, always building needed skills while improving your leadership. Should you neglect your management base, it could undermine your future. You still must stay current in management, even though you have mastered the Leadership Formula and woven the elements into your style. Balance, again, is the key for making the essentials of leadership work for you.

With these simple cautions in mind, you are prepared to become the kind of leader/manager or manager/leader you want to be.

Give it your best shot!

* The primary use for the Leadership Formula (Leadership Strategic Model star) is as a guide for personal growth. **SUMMARY**
* The Formula (or Model) can be used to pinpoint areas of weakness for those already in leadership roles.
* Understanding your own leadership style will help you understand why other people act as they do.
* If your style is based on a direct approach, you set clear goals, give specific directions, and supervise the progress of your followers.
* Individuals who take a permissive approach to leadership let subordinates determine whatever path they wish to take; if everything is left to chance, leadership may become nonexistent.
* Leaders who are "coaches" practice a support approach by assur-

ing two-way communication; they help followers reach goals through team involvement.

* Readers can use the elements of the Leadership Formula to rate the leadership performance of others.
* Leaders (more than managers) are vulnerable to dissenters.
* Those who desire to become leaders should do so within their own comfort zones or personality frameworks.
* Leaders must maintain their management competence.
* Self-improvement begins with your desire to take action to maximize your leadership style.
* It is best to work toward a good balance—one that works for you—when applying the Leadership Formula and developing the essentials of leadership.

Aaron and Rose have been stuck in their management positions for over three years. They agree that the best way to move up is to put more leadership into their styles.

Rose plans to do this in a dramatic fashion. Having carefully analyzed her power of influence, she has decided to work hard on two parts of the Leadership Strategic Model and ignore the others.

First, she is going to tighten her discipline line a notch and maintain it with force. She feels it is time to demonstrate her leadership more emphatically. Second, through more group interaction, she intends to generate a more positive force within her department. She intends to keep it going by becoming more positive personally, more active, and more assertive in all her associations with others. She is going to be center stage at all times.

Aaron, more conservative and cautious by nature, feels that each of the Leadership Formula elements is equally important and wishes to achieve balance. He is fearful that if he tightens his authority line without first making sure that his reward system is effective, he might get into trouble. He is also fearful that if he suddenly becomes more of a positive force, the reaction from others might be counterproductive. He intends to gradually upgrade himself in all of the Formula elements without calling attention to himself. He feels that gradual development will be most effective in getting him a promotion.

Which strategy do you support? Defend your position. (The authors' reactions are given in the back of the book.)

Case 20: Prediction

Janice is self-confident, capable, and ambitious—a high-energy person. She never does anything halfway; it is all or nothing. Janice switches from one self-improvement project to another at frequent intervals. Everyone envies her energy, enthusiasm, and creativity. Her colleagues have noticed, however, that her follow-through is not always what it should be. There is little structure in her department and her employees are the most undisciplined in the firm.

Jill is also self-confident, capable, and ambitious—and a planner. She goes about everything in a methodical, deliberate manner. Her follow-through is excellent. She shows great attention to detail. Most of her coworkers admire her low-key approach. Some, however, feel she needs to become more of a self-starter and to provide greater recognition to those who work for her.

Both Janice and Jill, after attending a leadership workshop, wish to incorporate the Leadership Formula into their respective styles.

What kind of success would you predict for Janice? Jill? Why? Which approach—direct, permissive, support—best describes the style of each? (The authors' responses are in the back of the book.)

Mark each statement True (T) or False (F).   **Self-Test**

_____ 1. Most managers can expect personal help from their superiors to maximize their leadership styles.

_____ 2. If you know the actions that contribute to your leadership style, you can better understand the approach others take.

_____ 3. Those in nonleadership positions also can apply the Leadership Formula for self-improvement.

_____ 4. A major personality change is required to put more leadership into your management style.

_____ 5. A person should not attempt to use the Leadership Strategic Model to rate the leadership effectiveness of others.

_____ 6. The Leadership Formula is a reference point that communicates the essence of leadership.

_____ 7. Leaders whose act as coaches are following the support approach in their leadership style.

_____ 8. Because all the Leadership Formula elements are interrelated, it can be dangerous to emphasize one at the expense of another.

_____ 9. Leadership development starts with a desire for self-improvement; taking action is the next critical step.

_____10. If you are successful in putting more leadership into your style, your superiors and subordinates will notice a positive difference in your behavior.

Turn to the back of the book to check your answers.

TOTAL CORRECT _____

Authors' Responses to Case Problems

The leadership cases at the end of each chapter were designed to be springboards for individual thinking and discussion purposes. There are no "right" answers to any of them and different points of view should be encouraged.

The following responses are offered as the authors' opinions, based upon their investigation and interviews. These responses should serve only as a guide to the independent thinking of the reader and the discussion leader.

Professor Adams deserves support on the basis that good management practices are essential to good leadership. The point is well taken, however, that management professors might spend too much time on management and not enough on leadership. Their prejudices might show so much than nonbusiness students might drop the course. You can also build a case that nonmanagement professors might be able to see the total concept more clearly from where they stand. This would put them in the position to introduce experiences and cases of a more general nature.

CASE 1: CONTROVERSY

Both Elgin and Samantha start from excellent positions. Elgin, with his management expertise, should be able to make a quick and easy transition, providing he can move away from management and concentrate on leadership. Samantha, because of her leadership experience, may grasp the management skills and fundamentals sooner because she knows they will help her be a better leader. The authors, in this case, go along with Samantha because they feel that Elgin will fight leadership ideas every inch of the way. He will probably be more interested in defending the accepted value of management instead of taking a fresh look at leadership. Samantha, on the other hand, will accept them and weave them into her style without apparent conflict or indecision.

CASE 2: OPINION

CASE 3:
HIGH PRODUCER?

From the limited data provided, the authors favor Gene in the short term because he is a strong manager. Maureen shows substantial long-term potential, providing she develops her management and leadership potential. Her high energy level is a signal her leadership potential may be above that of Gene. Gene, of course, with his management foundation, can measurably increase productivity through stronger leadership.

CASE 4:
OPPORTUNITY

Leaving Ms. Preston in operations is easy to defend. It would appear she is a leadership role model as she circulates within the branch system. In this capacity, she would be difficult to place. Providing Ms. Preston has teaching talents, the idea of having her do in-house leadership training is excellent. Her impact could be extended. If the board makes this decision, the new director of human resources should be encouraged to work closely with Ms. Preston so the leadership gap within the organization can be closed.

CASE 5:
CONFLICT

The authors support the premise that if an individual learns the fundamentals of leadership in one environment, he or she should be able to transfer them to another situation. If Greg learned and practiced some fundamentals (like those presented in the Leadership Formula) in the military, he should have little trouble adapting them to a banking environment. It would appear that Greg is confused between leadership style and fundamentals. He may be having trouble because he is attempting to transfer an authoritative military style to a participatory situation. The fundamentals would fit both styles. As Vicki suggests, if a student learns the leadership basics in the classroom, he or she should be able to take them into any environment.

CASE 6:
POTENTIAL

The authors, naturally, give their support to Joan. Bob seems to feel he must take his winning style completely apart and rebuild it to incorporate the fundamentals. This is not the case. Bob can weave one or more fundamentals into his style without disrupting it. As he does this, it may be necessary to make minor adjustments and modifications, but that is as far as it may need to go. He will, however, improve and strengthen his present style because he will fill in the weak spots in his previous emphasis on fundamentals. Put another way, his effective style will improve because it will be based upon a stronger foundation. When Bob senses the difference between style and substance, his fears should dissipate.

CASE 7:
IMPROVEMENT

A formal course in public speaking or professional communication would probably provide Ms. Blake with the most help—especially if she took the course seriously, became involved, and stayed with it to the end. Additional live-audience experiences and practice with her video equipment would also help. It would also be beneficial for Ms. Blake to study other speakers and improve her skills through comparative analysis.

Both Celine and Matthew should seriously consider an MBA, but augment the program with one or more demanding communication courses. If possible, they should find a MBA program that includes pure communication courses as well as specialty courses (presentation skills, media, etc.).

CASE 8: ENHANCEMENT

All leaders who incorporate MRT into their style will automatically strengthen their leadership because they will have better contact with their organizations and a better knowledge of their employee needs. Ralph's compassion for others should make the adoption and application of MRT easy and more effective. Still, it is doubtful that this will happen, because he is not enthusiastic about it. Perhaps he does not sense a need to be a stronger leader or build better relationships with his employees. He seems to be satisfied with things as they are. Unless he comes to the realization that MRT could help him serve his employees better, nothing will happen.

CASE 9: COMPASSION

The best way to convince yourself of the value of MRT is to actually use it and measure the results. Therefore, chances are good that after Mr. Nelson and Mr. Castelletti work out a better reward system between themselves, Mr. Castelletti will become more enthusiastic. Mr. Castelletti's fear is understandable but not justified. It is a comfortable approach to improving relationships and can be used in any environment with any style. Mr. Castelletti needs to be convinced that it will work as well for him, using his own approach and his own words, and that it is not just a technique for psychologists. Receiving the right rewards is as important to truckers as anyone else.

CASE 10: FEAR

Gloria may be a little optimistic about her chances of turning Jane into a forceful leader, but it is a real possibility. Assertiveness training, personal development, and leadership seminars have demonstrated leaders can be "made." No one is born to be either a follower or a leader. This is not to say that anyone can become President of the United States just because they want to, but anyone who wants to be a leader can become one—and at a high level—depending on how hard they work at it and the degree to which they are willing to change. Jane, with Gloria's help, can develop the courage to stand up to others. She can learn to apply structure. The very fact that Gloria sees Jane in the role as her assistant is an indication that the potential is there.

CASE 11: COURAGE

Captain Guerro builds an excellent case that MRT and structure are not only compatible but mutually dependent. One works much better when

CASE 12: COMPATIBILITY

the other is present. A good balance of MRT and structure is perhaps even more true in the military than in less structured environments. In short, the more structure required, the more MRT is needed. Any military officer who can build a disciplined defense unit on a sound human relations platform is going to be a successful, respected leader.

The authors are totally convinced that the more a leader uses MRT, the easier and more effective the application of structure becomes. When subordinates receive the right rewards, they will accept structure because structure protects and continues the reward system. Both parties come out ahead. Of course, it is possible to be a compassionate leader in the modern military establishment.

CASE 13:
VIEWPOINT

Both viewpoints deserve support. Mr. Bello makes a strong point when he states there is a time lag between when decisions are made and when they are judged good or bad. Ms. James is also right when she states that a poor decision can come home to haunt a leader. There is always a risk, as every long-term leader has discovered, of decision backfire. Most leaders who have had input into the Leadership Formula agree with the importance of decision making; some suggested that decision making be given even more weight among the basic foundations. "The buck stops here" is a common phrase of leaders meaning that they know they live with the pressure of making decisions. Decision-making responsibility may dissuade many people from assuming leadership roles.

CASE 14:
DECISION

The authors strongly support the two trustees who believe it is most difficult to verify the decision-making ability of an applicant. As for submitting their records in advance, it is naive to think that they would not construct them to make themselves look good. The best way to gain insight into the decision-making capabilities of an applicant is to ask some of the following questions during the interview stage: "What role does decision making have in leadership?" "Why do you feel you are a good decision maker?" "What is the process you follow in making decisions? How have you tested it?" Answers to these questions should be most revealing and provide the interview board with the data it needs on this vital subject. Is the board placing too much emphasis on decision making? Absolutely not! The destiny of any organization is determined more by the quality of decisions than by any other factor.

CASE 15:
SUB-MISSIONS

It would be ideal if the leader of a sizable organization could create and communicate an overriding purpose (mission) so powerful and involving that it would preclude the need for separate departmental missions. In such situations, smaller or sub-missions might even do more harm than good. It might be a mistake, however, to say that work teams within the framework of a large organization should not have the opportunity to develop missions of their own. A primary purpose of a mission is to make a group or team more cohesive, provide direction, and furnish an identity. If smaller organizations like churches, sports teams, and volunteer groups can benefit from the creation of a mission as opposed to a goal, then it makes sense that branches, divisions, or departments within a large organization could also benefit. The authors support both views, but lean in the direction of the professor, because it would be a mistake to discourage departmental managers from giving serious thought to a mission for their employees. What if the top leader(s) of the organization has (have) failed to come up with a motivating mission?

CASE 16: INVOLVEMENT

Although Ms. Loring states she believes in participatory management, in this case her plan appears to be too heavy-handed to work. Leaders at all levels must want to come up with missions. When it becomes a requirement, it can become a prefunctory assignment with no meaning. It is the position of the authors that missions should come from *inside* leaders, not outside. Missions and leaders must reflect the needs (rewards) of the members of the group and provide vision beyond current goals. In some departments, a team mission may not be possible. Therefore, to require each department manager to come up with a slogan may do more damage than good. The plan might work, however, on a volunteer basis. At least a few departments might create missions that would be meaningful. It is just not realistic to think this could happen in (or be beneficial for) all departments.

CASE 17: CHARISMA

Although charisma can be an irreplaceable asset to a leader, especially in the political arena, it is not essential. A leader with charisma may communicate a positive force more easily, but a positive force can be established without it, as Rebecca states. In fact, some leaders lean so heavily on charisma that they ignore the other more powerful elements necessary to establish a positive force. It would be difficult, perhaps impossible, to build a case that a positive attitude is a charismatic characteristic. Charisma is a mix of traits that communicates a certain magic to followers; attitude is the way the person looks at things mentally. Team members respond enthusiastically to any leader who has a positive attitude, perhaps because they want to believe in their leaders and the direction they are being asked to take. A charismatic leader may provide excitement, but a positive leader provides hope. The combination of both is, of course, ideal.

CASE 18: COMMUNICATION

It would appear that Ms. Grey may be overestimating the importance of communication in transmitting J.B.'s positive force; on the other hand, Mr. Fisher may be underestimating the role of public relations. It is impossible to say how far the positive force of a leader can be transmitted personally and when the communication network should take over. The leader of a small group (Boy Scout leader) may not need any help from a formal communication system, but the President of the United States needs all the help available. The balance required between the two is probably determined by the size of the group and the number of members who may be some distance away. A utility with 9,000 employees certainly needs a two-level, two-way communication network if the positive force of the leader is to reach everyone. By the same token, Ms. Grey is lucky to have a leader who does so much on his own.

CASE 19: EMPHASIS

The authors defend Aaron and his balanced strategy. Only through the integration of all foundations into one's style will full benefits occur. Overemphasis of one or more foundations can be dangerous because of the interrelationships between all. Taking this stand, however, does not mean that Rose will not benefit. It is possible (not covered in the scenario) that Rose is already excellent at MRT and her decision-making capabilities are high. In this case, she is filling in weak spots; and her strategy will work. For most people, however, Aaron's strategy is best.

CASE 20: PREDICTION

Weaving the Leadership Formula into one's style requires follow-through if success is to be achieved. Thus, it would appear that Jill has a decided edge over Janice. People who make a big thing about behavioral changes often put on a good show, but no permanent change takes place—a possibility with Janice. Jill's low-key approach may also offer benefits from a human relations point of view. Her coworkers may not sense ahead of time that she is becoming a strong leader, so no negative or jealous waves from others may develop. The danger of "coming on too strong" is always present when behavioral changes are made. Putting more leadership into your style should be a slow, sound, and permanent process for the best results.

The case does not provide enough detail to determine the approaches each woman practices. However, Janice probably leans more toward the permissive approach; although she has some of the support approach qualities. Jill probably leans toward the direct approach.

Answers to Self-Tests

CHAPTER 1
1. T
2. T
3. T
4. T (This is highly recommended.)
5. T
6. F 7.   T
8. T (Becoming a better manager also enhances leadership.)
9. T
10. F (It's the balance that counts.)

CHAPTER 2
1. T
2. T
3. T
4. F
5. F
6. F (Leaders are known for this.)
7. T
8. T
9. T
10. T

CHAPTER 3
1. T
2. T
3. T
4. F (Both should be capable of achieving results.)
5. T
6. T
7. F (It is an extremely critical part.)
8. T
9. T

10. T (Leadership is multifaceted and cannot be adequately explained in a single sentence or paragraph.)

CHAPTER 4
1. T
2. F (Both are important.)
3. F
4. T
5. T
6. F (The scale is only one signal. Besides, many successful leaders overcome early communication handicaps.)
7. T
8. F (They are counseling techniques)
9. T
10. T

CHAPTER 5
1. T
2. T (This is a premise of the theory.)
3. T
4. F (They provide too few, and often the wrong ones.)
5. T (This is a primary advantage of MRT.)
6. F (The ultimate franchise to lead comes from followers.)
7. T
8. T
9. F (Like anything else, it requires commitment and practice.)
10. T

CHAPTER 6
1. T (This is a very strong recommendation for MRT.)
2. T
3. F (Role power comes from the position one occupies.)
4. F (They normally expand personality power and diminish role power.)
5. F (They often do not have a good balance of power.)
6. T
7. T
8. F (Very few successful leaders have recognizable charisma.)
9. F (Leaders make greater use of personality power.)
10. T

CHAPTER 7
1. T
2. F
3. T
4. F (A prescribed, logical pattern is recommended, however.)

5. T
6. T
7. F (teams may produce a better decision, but seldom faster.)
8. T
9. F
10. F (Lack of time forces many gut decisions.)

CHAPTER 8
1. F (A mission is at a higher level, less practical, etc.)
2. F (A mission helps create and sustain a leader's power of influence.)
3. T
4. T
5. T
6. F
7. F (Usually, articulation is the most difficult.)
8. F
9. T
10. T

CHAPTER 9
1. T
2. T
3. F (Everyone has a certain capacity; but some more than others.)
4. T
5. F (A positive force is particularly dependent upon personality power.)
6. T
7. T
8. T
9. T
10. F

CHAPTER 10
1. F (It is a do-it-yourself project.)
2. T
3. T
4. F
5. F
6. T
7. T
8. T (This is especially true when it comes to applying more structure without MRT.)
9. T
10. T

LEADERSHIP EFFECTIVENESS SCALE

INSTRUCTIONS

Here are thirty-six (36) practices commonly demonstrated by acknowledged leaders. Read each statement carefully. Decide the extent to which each practice is characteristic of the person being rated. Circle the appropriate number to the right of each practice.

(Name of Person Being Rated)	Strongly Agree	Somewhat Agree	Somewhat Disagree	Strongly Disagree
The person being rated:				
1. Keeps followers fully informed.	4	3	2	1
2. Expresses thoughts clearly and forcefully.	4	3	2	1
3. Speaks well from a platform.	4	3	2	1
4. Is a good listener.	4	3	2	1
5. Attracts others to want to hear what he/she has to say.	4	3	2	1
6. Communicates a sense of "being in charge."	4	3	2	1
7. Develops employees into followers.	4	3	2	1
8. Demonstrates compassion for others.	4	3	2	1
9. Provides rewards that are important to followers.	4	3	2	1
10. Strives to win by allowing followers to win also.	4	3	2	1
11. Attracts others to want to join his/her group.	4	3	2	1
12. Has the full backing of all those who work under her/him.	4	3	2	1
The person being rated:				
13. Provides enough structure to create a cohesive feeling among his/her subordinates.	4	3	2	1
14. Establishes an authority line that is clear, consistent, and appropriate for the situation.	4	3	2	1
15. Utilizes role, personality, and knowledge power in a balanced, effective manner.	4	3	2	1
16. Gets tough when necessary.	4	3	2	1
17. Is respected by subordinates when authority is used.	4	3	2	1
18. Uses the power that he/she has with firmness but also with sensitivity.	4	3	2	1
19. Consults with others before making important decisions.	4	3	2	1

	Strongly Agree	Somewhat Agree	Somewhat Disagree	Strongly Disagree
20. Has a strong track record for making solid decisions.	4	3	2	1
21. Follows a logical pattern in making decisions.	4	3	2	1
22. Stages and communicates decisions with pride and decisiveness.	4	3	2	1
23. Is able to admit mistakes when he/she makes them.	4	3	2	1
24. Faces up to and makes hard decisions.	4	3	2	1
25. Always maintains an upbeat, positive attitude.	4	3	2	1
26. Articulates an inspiring mission to all employees/followers.	4	3	2	1
27. Generates a feeling of pride and higher productivity in followers.	4	3	2	1
28. Ties short-term work goals to inspirational missions.	4	3	2	1
29. Makes work more enjoyable.	4	3	2	1
30. Shares both large and small victories with followers.	4	3	2	1
31. Gets others caught up in his/her positive force.	4	3	2	1
32. Creates an active tempo that others want to emulate.	4	3	2	1
33. Reflects a positive attitude during difficult or tough times.	4	3	2	1
34. Is highly energetic and refuses to be "desk bound."	4	3	2	1

	Strongly Agree	Somewhat Agree	Somewhat Disagree	Strongly Disagree
The person being rated:				
35. Inspires others to be all they can be.	4	3	2	1
36. If she/he resigned, others would want to follow.	4	3	2	1

Turn to page 174 for scoring instructions.

LEADERSHIP EFFECTIVENESS SCALE SCORING INSTRUCTIONS FOR SELF-RATING EXERCISE (PAGE 151)

Determine the point value for your response to each item and enter it in the score column. Total the scores for all six items in each category to obtain the CATEGORY SCORE. Then enter the scores for each category in the SCORE column of the summary section. Total the category scores to obtain the LEADERSHIP EFFECTIVENESS SCORE.

Leader as EFFECTIVE COMMUNICATOR

Item:	SA	SWA	SWD	SD	Score
1.	4	3	2	1	_____
2.	4	3	2	1	_____
3.	4	3	2	1	_____
4.	4	3	2	1	_____
5.	4	3	2	1	_____
6.	4	3	2	1	_____
Category Score =					_____

Leader who EMPOWERS FOLLOWERS

Item:	SA	SWA	SWD	SD	Score
7.	4	3	2	1	_____
8.	4	3	2	1	_____
9.	4	3	2	1	_____
10.	4	3	2	1	_____
11.	4	3	2	1	_____
12.	4	3	2	1	_____
Category Score =					_____

Leader with POWER OF INFLUENCE

Item:	SA	SWA	SWD	SD	Score
13.	4	3	2	1	_____
14.	4	3	2	1	_____
15.	4	3	2	1	_____
16.	4	3	2	1	_____
17.	4	3	2	1	_____
18.	4	3	2	1	_____
Category Score =					_____

Leader as DECISION MAKER

Item:	SA	SWA	SWD	SD	Score
19.	4	3	2	1	_____
20.	4	3	2	1	_____
21.	4	3	2	1	_____
22.	4	3	2	1	_____
23.	4	3	2	1	_____
24.	4	3	2	1	_____
Category Score =					_____

Leader as VISIONARY

Item:	SA	SWA	SWD	SD	Score
25.	4	3	2	1	_____
26.	4	3	2	1	_____
27.	4	3	2	1	_____
28.	4	3	2	1	_____
29.	4	3	2	1	_____
30.	4	3	2	1	_____
Category Score =					_____

Leader as POSITIVE FORCE

Item:	SA	SWA	SWD	SD	Score
31.	4	3	2	1	_____
32.	4	3	2	1	_____
33.	4	3	2	1	_____
34.	4	3	2	1	_____
35.	4	3	2	1	_____
36.	4	3	2	1	_____
Category Score =					_____

SCORE BOX

Category	Score
Leader as Effective Communicator	☐
Leader who Empowers Followers	☐
Leader with Power of Influence	☐
Leader as Decision Maker	☐
Leader as Visionary	☐
Leader as Positive Force	☐
LEADERSHIP EFFECTIVENESS SCORE	☐

144–120 = strong leader, 119–100 = good leader,
99–80 = fair leader.

LEADERSHIP EFFECTIVENESS SCALE SCORING INSTRUCTIONS FOR EVALUATOR RATING EXERCISE (PAGE 170)

Determine the point value your evaluator gave you on each item and enter it in the score column. Total the scores for all six items in each category to obtain the CATEGORY SCORE. Then enter the scores for each category in the SCORE column of the summary section. Total the category scores to obtain the LEADERSHIP EFFECTIVENESS SCORE.

Leader as EFFECTIVE COMMUNICATOR

Item:	SA	SWA	SWD	SD	Score
1.	4	3	2	1	_____
2.	4	3	2	1	_____
3.	4	3	2	1	_____
4.	4	3	2	1	_____
5.	4	3	2	1	_____
6.	4	3	2	1	_____
Category Score =					_____

Leader who EMPOWERS FOLLOWERS

Item:	SA	SWA	SWD	SD	Score
7.	4	3	2	1	_____
8.	4	3	2	1	_____
9.	4	3	2	1	_____
10.	4	3	2	1	_____
11.	4	3	2	1	_____
12.	4	3	2	1	_____
Category Score =					_____

Leader with POWER OF INFLUENCE

Item:	SA	SWA	SWD	SD	Score
13.	4	3	2	1	_____
14.	4	3	2	1	_____
15.	4	3	2	1	_____
16.	4	3	2	1	_____
17.	4	3	2	1	_____
18.	4	3	2	1	_____
Category Score =					_____

Leader as DECISION MAKER

Item:	SA	SWA	SWD	SD	Score
19.	4	3	2	1	_____
20.	4	3	2	1	_____
21.	4	3	2	1	_____
22.	4	3	2	1	_____
23.	4	3	2	1	_____
24.	4	3	2	1	_____
Category Score =					_____

Leader as VISIONARY					
Item:	SA	SWA	SWD	SD	Score
25.	4	3	2	1	_____
26.	4	3	2	1	_____
27.	4	3	2	1	_____
28.	4	3	2	1	_____
29.	4	3	2	1	_____
30.	4	3	2	1	_____
Category Score =					_____

Leader as POSITIVE FORCE					
Item:	SA	SWA	SWD	SD	Score
31.	4	3	2	1	_____
32.	4	3	2	1	_____
33.	4	3	2	1	_____
34.	4	3	2	1	_____
35.	4	3	2	1	_____
36.	4	3	2	1	_____
Category Score =					_____

SCORE BOX

Category	**Score**
Leader as Effective Communicator	☐
Leader who Empowers Followers	☐
Leader with Power of Influence	☐
Leader as Decision Maker	☐
Leader as Visionary	☐
Leader as Positive Force	☐
LEADERSHIP EFFECTIVENESS SCORE	☐

144–120 = strong leader, 119–100 = good leader,
99–80 = fair leader.

Index